THE STATE OF
BEING LOVE

STEPS TO INCREASE YOUR VIBRATION
FOR A JOY FILLED LIFE

LEEZA DONATELLA

Printed in the United States of America

First Edition – November 2015

Paperback
ISBN-13: 978-0-9911007-6-7
ISBN-10: 099110076X

Higher Roads Productions
Copyright © 2015

Dedication

To all the unpleasant experiences that made me
search for answers and methods that lead me to
the state of *Being Love*.

And to my sister Toni Ann,
who always believes in me.

THE STATE OF BEING LOVE

Contents

ABOUT THE AUTHOR

LeeZa lives a pretty amazing life, filled with extraordinary experiences and synchronicity. She's trekked through the Amazon, climbed atop Machu Picchu in the Andes, has been invited to join Shamans in Ayahuasca ceremonies and meditated in the middle of Brazil while helping charitable organizations. She achieved her undergraduate degree at 19 years young, worked in consultancy for many years, ending her corporate stay as a technology VP for a global financial institution.

Today she speaks to both U.S. and International audiences about what inspires and motivates us, causes us stress and ways to balance, release and heal. The philosophy LeeZa teaches is about getting to and maintaining the state she calls **being love**.

LeeZa's been involved with alternative modalities since her early twenties, having worked alongside many other healers and masters. She's been fortunate to have been shown Shamanic practices during her travels and volunteering in South America. Her studies have included Bio-Energy, Japanese Reiki, Anapana and Vipassana Meditation, Chakra Balancing and Harmonization, Oils and Herbalism,

Reflexology and Acupressure, Cognitive Behavior Therapy (CBT) and the Emotional Freedom Technique (EFT).

"I've never felt more alive as I strive to help people move forward. I wish you all the LOVE in the Universe. Open your heart to let it in, sigh and breathe the sweet fragrance of the deliciousness of life."

LeeZa Donatella

See www.leezadonatella.com
for more information.

INTRODUCTION

There was a period in my life when I worked in the corporate world, working most of the past 20 years in private consultancy. As I put my fingers to the keyboard to write this book, I was reminded of the time when I made more money than I had time to spend. It was 1998-2000 and I was in high demand as companies were offering decent hourly rates as incentives to good consultants as the Y2K scare was in full swing. I worked tirelessly 80+hour weeks managing technology projects as the dreaded January 1st 2000 deadline approached.

When all was said and done, Y2K was not the big deal so many analysts made it out to be. The world did not stop in its tracks and business went on as usual.

My consultancy now complete, I took a long deserved and overdue break to recharge and spend some of the money that I had accumulated in my checking account, more than enough for my dream car, a Porsche 911 Cabriolet.

I strolled into the dealership knowing exactly what I wanted. I sat in that cherry red baby, the leather bucket seats forming perfectly around my round derrière. The salesman white knuckled the passenger grab bar during my test drive, as I hugged the curves in the road at the perfect angle and accelerated, just shy of losing control. When we returned, I told him that I was going to go to lunch and would contact him later that day.

Okay, so some of you reading this are probably thinking to yourself, *'Must be nice, what the heck is she complaining about?'* I'm not disagreeing with you. I have plenty of horrific stories I can share as well that would incite sympathy and empathy, but this is not one of them. I seized an opportunity, worked my butt off non-stop for 2 years and I was ready for my reward. From the couple of cars that I had purchased in the past, my process was to do my research, know what I wanted before walking into the dealership, test drive the car, then negotiate a price and drive it off the lot. For some reason though, today would be different.

I went to a nearby diner, ordered a BLT and sat there, twirling the straw in my ice tea. I thought about this purchase and assumed my hesitation was due to the fact that the car was over $100,000. But this was the car I had always dreamed of, so what was it that was causing me so much angst?

I opened up a small note book I kept in my purse, doodling on one of the pages, unable to take more than one bite of my sandwich. My stomach was not unsettled, but there was something else going on. It wasn't the money, for I had cash. I was not second guessing if it would be wiser to make another choice. That has never been how I operated.

Then it hit me like a ton of bricks.

I knew that if I bought this car, I would be ecstatic for a week or two, but then what?

I realized that buying that car was just going to be a pacifier, although an expensive flashy one, but was not going to fill the void that I had.

The epiphany I had that day was that I was living in what I now term a lower vibrational frequency that for now, let's call fear.

All this time I was working hard and obtaining goals, climbing the proverbial ladder adding additional status symbols like pins on a vest, only to realize that nothing *up there* was anything different than where I came from. Yes, you heard me, I figured out that my true worth and value was not measured by a societal derived status symbol or gained through material means.

I didn't buy the car that day, but decided instead a few weeks later to take a 3 month journey backpacking through parts of South America, following the life of ancient tribes that inhabited the area.

It's taken years of self-analyzation, studying and working alongside other masters to come to the theories to get to the state I call **being love**. It is these theories and practices that I am now sharing with all of you.

1

How People Live Today

I speak to audiences in the US and abroad and receive a ton of correspondence about how people are feeling and how they view themselves.

Overall, people are just not happy. They lack that elated feeling each day that I've been able to achieve, continually living with blinders on, oblivious to a more delicious life that's right in front of them.

Some people live most of their lives entangled in the rat race, striving to get to the top of the corporate ladder, thinking that once they achieve all the goals they set out for themselves, they'll experience that joy. Others toil tirelessly at self-employed or other types of businesses, to keep up with the Joneses. Still more live in a bubble of defeat, blanketed by misery and fear.

I'm not saying that there's anything wrong with money and nice things. I love money and nice things, but neither has value when it comes to inner joy.

If you can relate to any of the above, then you're looking for joy and happiness in external places. It's like a game of hide and seek and you haven't figured out yet that you're just looking in the wrong place and that's why you haven't found it yet.

I know that when God put us on this planet, it was not to live 60, 70, 80 or more years filled with hatred, anger, sadness or guilt. We're all loving beings and have something to offer others, especially the most important being in our lives, ourselves.

Some people are brought up to believe that there's something wrong with them, that they're missing some crucial quality. Perhaps there were a couple of people that you can think of who may have acted a certain way toward you or said a few words in your earlier years that helped introduce a possible negative belief within *you*. We aren't born with negative beliefs. These all come from experiences and they shape us as we define ourselves within these constraints, these limitations.

These are just a few examples of statements said to us by parents, guardians, authority figures and peers as young beings that shaped our core beliefs about ourselves and the world around us. How many of you have heard any of the following statements when you were growing up?

- Life is hard
- The world is a dangerous place
- You can't do anything right or you've disappointed me
- Children should be seen and not heard

Perhaps you met people over the years who made you feel bad about the way you looked, the way you dressed, your abilities, intelligence and popularity.

Am I blaming others for everything in our world that has gone wrong? Absolutely not. I take responsibility for my reaction, my perception and the beliefs that I chose to keep because we always have a choice about what we choose to believe.

Based on the above examples, the following beliefs that can take hold within us are:

- Every day is torturous
- I'm not going to try new things
- I'm not good enough
- I'm not smart enough
- I don't deserve it
- I'm a failure
- What I have to contribute has no value

And these beliefs can trigger negative emotions like loneliness and isolation, sadness, despair, low self-esteem and self-image, feelings of unworthiness, hopelessness, anger, guilt, envy, judgement, shame, cowardice, self-hate, bitterness and other emotions that *can* fill our minds from dawn until dusk.

What you may not know is that it also effects your vibration. I'll be talking more about vibration, but wanted to introduce this concept to you now as we begin to delve further.

~~~~~~~~~~~~~~~~~~~~~~

When I was living in Washington DC I had a friend named Denise. She was beautiful, smart and very spiritual, but she was continually plagued with picking the wrong guy. They would go out for a few months, take advantage of her generosity and then leave her crying at the curb. I was always there as the shoulder for her to cry on as she explained her latest escapades in great detail. We discovered an emerging pattern and although she was aware of it, because we didn't get to the root, that core belief that was the underlying reason that she continually picked losers, she was destined to do it again. And she did, over and over. Now that I'm older and hopefully a lot wiser, as information about Denise's issues began to emerge and after several long distance phone calls, we were able to get to the instance when she first took on the core belief that she was not good enough. We worked together to finally release this false belief and the corresponding blocked emotions.

~~~~~~~~~~~~~~~~~~~~~~~~

I speak more about blocked emotions and release later in the book, but want you to know that it is a piece to the puzzle of why people are having trouble living a joy filled life.

THE STATE OF BEING LOVE

2
WHAT IS VIBRATIONAL FREQUENCY?

All the atoms in all your cells vibrate at a particular vibration or frequency.

Science tells us that there are over 100 trillion atoms in each cell in your body, each one of them vibrating. Now here's where the definition gets expansive:

Each emotion that you experience has its own vibrational frequency and there is a correlation between your emotional state and your body's overall vibration.

So, if you take on this belief then you will also come to know that emotions are merely energy in motion with different emotions have different vibrations. Some have assigned numbers to the vibratory level of main emotions ranging from 0 to 1000. At the bottom of the scale are emotions like shame and guilt and toward the top of the scale are unconditional love and enlightenment. It is believed that most human's live in emotions that never rise above 150-200.[i]

I have not found anyone who can scientifically prove a way to associate a particular number with an emotion, but I do believe that there are certain key emotions that keep you in the **being love** state. I came up with an easy way to know which state you are in by using 2 categories when I speak to audiences. You are either in that state of **being love** or you're vibrating **something else**. When you're in the **being love** state, you feel great as you float within bliss and elation. When you vibrate in that **something else** state, you don't feel anything, or are consumed in the gamut of negative or fear-based emotions that have lower vibrational frequencies. They keep you from living a joy filled life.

One of the side benefits I noticed when in that higher vibrational range I call **being love**, has to do with the way we look. Have you ever noticed that when someone has lived a hard life they look prematurely old? I would always comment about the US president that when they went into office they had dark hair and before the end of the 2nd year they would all be completely grey.

Stress is, after all, emotional dis-stress that manifests physically in our bodies.

I'm not a scientist so I can't scientifically prove that the vibratory frequency in each of our cells are allowing them to decelerate or accelerate their rejuvenation process, based on emotional impacts, but if emotional distress causes us to age, why wouldn't emotional bliss increase the rejuvenation process?

For some people just this alone would increase their desire about learning more. What if you could get the benefit of feeling bliss and turn back the clock on aging? What a scrumptious thought!

Nicola Tesla said, "The day science begins to study nonphysical phenomena, it will make more progress in one decade than in all previous centuries of its existence."[ii]

~~~~~~~~~~~~~~~~~~~~~~~~

I noticed that I was looking younger in my photos and my skin looked better, but it wasn't until I received validation that this concept finally sunk in. I want to preface this with the fact that I did not change to a healthy diet. I love bacon and still could eat better and drink more water. But last year when I found an old photo album of my adventures in Peru from back in the 1990's, I took my favorite pictures and scanned them to digital, saving them to a folder on my PC. I was out for coffee with a girlfriend that I've known for a couple of years and the subject of Peru came up. Since a writer always has their PC with them in case inspiration strikes, I shared with her some of my Peru photos.

"I didn't know you were in Peru last year," she questioned.

"What?" I laughed. "That photo's about 20 years old."

She looked at me astonished stating that I hadn't aged a bit and in fact I look younger now than I did then. Although this is not why I wanted to get to that state of **being love**, just the thought of the possibility of this unknown side benefit, had me ecstatic. Had I discovered my own personal fountain of youth?

On the converse side, there was a period from 2005 through 2009 that I was miserable. It showed in my photos. It seemed that this was self-reversing as I learned to get back to and maintain a **being love** state.

~~~~~~~~~~~~~~~~~~~~~~~~

When we raise our vibration we change. Our world shifts into something so scrumptious and intoxicating that words cannot describe. And it also seems that we also change from the inside out.

~~~~~~~~~~~~~~~~~~~~~~~

THE STATE OF BEING LOVE

3

ABOUT FEAR

Fear will always keep you from realizing your potential of being love.

Fear is not just cowering in a corner doing nothing, but also encompasses many other emotions and behaviors. The term I use for this negativity is referring to them as fear-based lower vibrational frequencies. They're emotions that keep us from moving forward into that ***being love*** state. I refer to this state as vibrating ***something else*** in the previous chapter.

When a person is not in the ***being love*** state they can feel alone, disconnected, cut-off from the rest of the world, living in misery and suffer emotional and spiritual blocks that can even affect their physical health.

Below are a few emotions that make up fear-based lower vibrational frequencies that cause people to stay in that ***something else*** state:

Anger	Fear/Terror	Paranoid
Arrogance	Frustration	Pride
Anxiety	Greed	Possessive
Bitterness	Grief	Resentful
Competitiveness	Hatred	Self-righteousness
Conceit	Hopelessness	
Controlling	Indifference	Self-condemnation
Cruelty	Insecurity	Self-loathing
Depression	Jealousy	Self-pity
Desperation	Judgment	Shame
Disappointment	Loneliness	Stubbornness
Disconnected	Obsession	Un-forgivingness
Dominating	One-upness	Unhappiness
Egocentric	Overreaction	Vengefulness
Envy	Panic	Worry

The ***something else*** state lessens one's ability to live that beautiful life that is right there in front of them.

~~~~~~~~~~~~~~~~~~~~~~~~~

When I speak to audiences about lower vibrations, I'm reminded of someone I've known all of my life. He's very angry and is continually plagued with unpleasant situations. One that I will share with you was when he parked his car at a large discount store. It was one of those parking lots where everyone parks across from each other, heading into their parking spot on an angle. While he was inside, somehow, the brake disengaged on the car parked diagonally across from his vehicle, sending the other car rolling backward until it smashed into the side door of his van, causing several thousand dollars' worth of damage.

This is not of course an isolated incident, as I hear so many stories of things that seem to go wrong for him. Unfortunately that only strengthens his negative attitude about life.

~~~~~~~~~~~~~~~~~~~~~~~~~

I believe that people that continually live in a state of negativity, that state I call ***something else***, seem to continue to experience negative in their lives.

Take time to look at the list of all the fear-based lower vibrational frequencies that I've listed in this chapter and see if you find yourself living in one or more of them most of your day. If so, then it's time to make some changes.

4

LIVING IN LACK

Ah the dreaded lack that shows itself in the emotional state of many a person. When one lives in lack, absolutely nothing will ever be enough to satisfy them, no matter how much money, material gain or status they acquire.

From an emotional perspective, people who live in lack are looking to fill a void in their lives by some obsession. Perhaps it's amassing things, an obsession with material wealth or collections. I find that people with addictions to substances and even sex often fall within this category. And they find it hard to let go of what they obtain or their obsession. The problem is that once the high they receive wears off, they're back to feelings of unhappiness and emptiness.

Happiness and joy do not come in an external package with a pretty bow. As previously mentioned, I like nice things, flashy cars, status and spicy lovers, but once I realized that they are put in our path just to make our lives more comfortable, it was very easy for me to let go when it was time to release them and move on. Why? Because I do not define myself by what's external.

~~~~~~~~~~~~~~~~~~~~~~~~~

I was with someone for 6 years. Collectively in the 5th year of our marriage we were at the point where we were both making good financial livings. It was then that I realized a core problem. Nothing was ever going to be enough to satisfy this man, because he was living in lack. The more money we amassed, the more he spent. I used to call it supersizing, since everything he purchased had to come from a top designer down to the bed sheets and his underwear. These objects were part of the prestigious badge that defined his success. He continually had to have the best and newest technological gadget, bigger televisions, an upgraded computer when his was less than 1.5 years old, as well as the most expensive plates, silverware and crystal.

1 car would never do, he had to have 3 of his own: one sports car, 1 SUV and 1 classic car project. With the 1 vehicle I had that would make 4, just for the 2 of us. Toward the end of the relationship I was burnt out from the stress of the corporate hours, deadlines and

office politics. When I approached him stating that I needed a well-deserved break, he adamantly said no.

It was later that year, after time spent speaking with counselors that I decided to dissolve the marriage. He wanted to fight me on everything, even though it was *my* earnings that bought most of what we had. I walked away from all the material wealth in search of a better, brighter and happier future, toward the state of **being love**.

~~~~~~~~~~~~~~~~~~~~~~~

Living in lack is just another sign that there's something wrong, an emotional block that's keeping joy and happiness out of reach. So instead of reacting out of lack, think about why you are reaching for that 3rd drink after work to help you forget about what so-and-so said about you today, or buying that shiny new gadget. Be honest with yourself and decide why you have this urge.

If the answer is that something is lacking in your life, then you have just taken a step toward realizing a possible solution.

THE STATE OF BEING LOVE

5

Moving Away from Misery

If I've learned nothing over the decades that I've been on Earth, the one thing I know is that it's much better to remain a positive upbeat person regardless of the situation, than a miserable Mable. When I speak to audiences I know that they've found me because they're ready to move forward. All I do is provide a little guidance and some tools and they're making strides and moving mountains in no time.

It tugs at my heart when I encounter people, especially those I care about, who dwell in their own fear-based lower vibrational frequencies as they continue to vibrate lower with no desire to move away from them. They wear their misery like a comfortable old tattered blanket or use it as a shield forged in steel.

For those of you who are still clinging to misery, I hear you and know that it can be frightening to let it go, especially since you may have incorporated your misery into your very being.

I often think of my own mother when I site examples. She lost *her* mother when she was only 18 years old. It tortured her every holiday as she was continually reminded of her loss and grief, instead of celebrating the people that were still in her life.

I've counseled many women who are still consumed by the anger from a divorce that happened decades ago. They are so comfortable living in their anger that they see red at the mere mention of their ex-spouses name. I've also met people around the globe from all walks of life who have dwelled in lower vibrations for so long that they can't remember what joy feels like. They are consumed with sadness, despair, anger, hatred, self-doubt, worry and fear. What they do not realize is that each moment we have the ability to move away from misery.

~~~~~~~~~~~~~~~~~~~~~~

When I talk about misery I'm reminded of a bright young man in his early 30's named Alec, who I met one cold winters evening at a Murder Mystery event that his friend was hosting. It was immediately apparent as we continued to speak, that he was absolutely miserable due to his own design, but his brilliance and knowledge base fascinated me. He had recently lost his job which sends most people into a temporary tailspin, but for Alec it was much more than that. He just didn't believe in anything positive about his life. I was not surprised when I found out that his car was ticketed and towed to an impound lot where he did not have the funds to retrieve it, followed by losing his place to live. Now residing in the unfinished basement at a relative's home on a ratty old cat pissed-stained couch, he had totally given up on life. I left for an appearance tour abroad and checked in on him. I know that we all have our own homework, but it doesn't make it any easier when you see someone you care about struggling. I'm not one of those people who forces my beliefs on others, so I took the hint to back off, offering assistance if he ever wanted to reach out. When I returned to the states several months later he was still in the same place in his life. I tried my best to provide encouragement, but he was so convinced that his only choice was to continue to live in misery, that he said *thank you* as he disagreed and politely called me delusional.

~~~~~~~~~~~~~~~~~~~~~~~

They say that misery loves company, but who wants to hang out in a room filled with miserable people? I certainly don't. Do you? I'm referring to those people who live in emotions that are in the lower vibrational frequencies, let's call them the Debbie Downer, the Complainer and the Poor Me. I'm sure that we all know at least one.

These are the people that when we see them we turn and quickly walk the other way before they recognize us. And when they come up on our caller ID, we have to determine if we take the call or let it go to voicemail. Why? Because we know that we'll be on the phone with them for over an hour and after the call finally ends, we feel drained and exhausted because we allow ourselves to get caught up in the drama of their lower vibrational energy.

~~~~~~~~~~~~~~~~~~~~~~~

I'll never forget when I enjoyed coffee with a friend who was going through a really tough time. He was angry, hated his job and was having issues in his relationship. I explained the state of **being love** to him and he turned to me replying, "Oh, that's not easy to keep that up."

"Really?" I responded. "Why not?"

"It's just too much work," he confessed.

"So let me get this straight," I commented. "Waking up, feeling awful, dragging yourself out of bed, hating your job and your life and thinking about who said something that made you feel bad yesterday, grimacing, complaining and going about your day, ready to rip someone's head off is *easier* than waking feeling good, thinking about nothing but that moment and smiling, singing and going about your day and greeting everyone you meet. Okay, so which seems like more work?"

He laughed for the first time in months as I presented a different perspective, then asked to hear more.

~~~~~~~~~~~~~~~~~~~~~~~~

Most people strive toward joy as if it's a reward to be obtained or bought. That's the problem. It's like the proverbial carrot being dangled in front of us with the promise of *someday*. And there are plenty of companies trying to sell that dream on that *someday* formula as if it's something you can buy, like a new dress, the perfect body or luxury car. The problem is that *someday* never comes. Why? Because it's always in the future. That's *their* plan, one that keeps us buying into the dream, but never obtaining the joyous

THE STATE OF BEING LOVE

outcome. And it's this formula that keeps people living in misery.

Like most if not all of you, I too have had periods in my life where I lived in what I call the misery of the mind. It's that place where you just survive, with each day blending into another. You're filled with every emotion that's not joy. I remember being angry, wallowing in self-pity and at times totally give up.

Joy, happiness and getting to the **being love** state is not going to come down and swat you on the behind and say, hey, here I am. It's a choice you make. And when you make the choice to move away from misery, you start to release those fear-based lower vibrational frequencies, what most call negative emotions and take a bite of the deliciousness of life.

And the biggest false belief out there is that it's impossible or extremely difficult. Admittedly, it may make you feel uncomfortable as you open up the chest with the rusty lock and start pulling out everything that is buried in there, but in the words of my father when he counseled me in my youth, "It's a piece of cake."

It's time to try a new way.

6
GUILT AND OBLIGATION

When I speak about guilt, I'm not talking about the kind of guilt that comes from committing a crime. I'm talking about times when you feel self-imposed guilt, for example, as you automatically get a pit in your stomach and feel awful when you're called into your manager's office, assuming that you've done something wrong. Maybe you been made to feel terrible by someone else as they tried to get you to do something.

If you have, then you've experienced the dreaded guilt trip, whether self-imposed or otherwise. This includes doing something when you're not feeling your best, going to places or events that you know you won't enjoy as well as associating with people that you may not want to interact with. It's because of the guilt trip that we end up caving, out of a sense of obligation.

I've seen this in extreme cases of arranged marriages or more subtle cases like Susan's. Although this happened over 40 years ago when Susan was no more than 5, it still stands out in her mind and struck a chord in me. It was early one Sunday. She had no temperature, but her head and stomach were aching. She told her mother that she wasn't feeling well enough to attend services that morning. Her mother swiftly turned and told this young girl that she had to go, and if she didn't get herself out of bed and get dressed right now, that she was going to hell. Susan complied, got dressed and went with her parents that day. At services her temperature spiked and she became ill, vomiting on her mother while sitting in the church.

Some of you may laugh at Susan's story as you think that her mother got what she deserved, for not believing her daughter. But the effect that it had on Susan was devastating. Even at 5 years old it was an embarrassing experience that still haunts her. It kept her attending functions that she absolutely hated, and dragged herself to work when she was very ill, out of a warped sense of obligation.

~~~~~~~~~~~~~~~~~~~~~~~

Understandably, as children we don't always have a say in family activities. We all know that a 5 year old making all the decisions would certainly be the mark of a dysfunctional household. But as adults though, we *are* entitled to make our own decisions.

Speaking to so many people with similar stories about guilt and a sense of obligation, made me realize that what is learned as young children becomes part of our overall belief system. We carry it around with us like a frayed handbag, continually doing what we don't want to out of guilt or a sense of obligation.

Growing up in an Italian household, I can relate to the art of the perfectly placed guilt trip. I loved my mother, but the guilt trips were dished out as frequently as the homemade pasta and sauce that Italian moms are famous for. For this sensitive kid, it was at times more than I could handle. It effected most of my young adult life as I continued to do things that provided me absolutely no enjoyment because I felt obligated to do so.

Doing something that you don't want to do, well that's ridiculous. Why should we as adults do things that we know that we won't enjoy? Yet we're conditioned to impose guilt on ourselves as if the people in our lives, like momma, are still standing over us, even when they're not. Another big factor is that the guilt, the emotion, vibrates much lower than other more pleasant feelings. It's far down the list from higher vibrational frequencies, like unconditional love. It is probably tied with shame at being the lowest of the fear-based lower vibrational frequencies.

When I was married, I loved that my then husband had a close tie with his family. After a while I discovered that my mother-in-law was obsessed with the time between Thanksgiving and New Year's Day. I termed it the Christmas frenzy, with more made up excuses for family get-togethers than was normal. All and all in that 4 week period there was a minimum of 12 family get-togethers. The first year of my marriage I went to all these events, but I was quick to realize that I would enjoy spending more time with my own family during the holidays. I loved my husband's parents, but I chose to graciously decline some of these invitations, allowing my husband to go and spend time with his family, while I spent time with mine. The guilt trips that were communicated through my husband about how I brought his mother to tears when I was not present were overwhelming. I got firsthand the flavor of the intensity of me choosing how I spent the precious few hours I had off from the traveling I was doing as part of my corporate job, each time I saw her.

Over the course of my marriage it was always less than 2 weeks in between visits to his parents. Yet every time I would see my mother-in-law, the first words from her mouth were, "It's been so long since we've seen you." I always smiled and let it roll, thinking of the guilt and obligation that she must have felt throughout her own life to attempt to use a guilt trip to make me feel awful, instead of being grateful for the time that we spent together.

What Can You Do?
Having had plenty of practice with this type of guilt, I decided approximately 10 or 15 years ago that I no longer needed this experience. I'm old enough and wise enough to know when I won't enjoy doing something. And if I'm not going to enjoy something, I just don't do it, **period**. And I don't feel one ounce of guilt based on my decision to only do what makes me happy.

If someone attempts to make me feel guilty, I just tell them, sorry, I don't do guilt anymore. I only do what makes me feel good, taking action on what provides me with pleasure. When I speak about pleasure, I'm not saying that I disregard the rules or disrespect people or organizations. So no, I don't go out of my way to walk into a church wearing a bikini singing

Madonna's 1980s hit *Like a Virgin.* This may not make me miss popular, but I am definitely miss happier, vibrating higher as a result.

So the next time someone attempts to guilt trip you, just smile, say no thank you and walk in the other direction, without reservation, regret, obligation or guilt. Hold your head high and vibrate only unconditional love.

7

SELF-WORTH AND SELF ESTEEM

Self-esteem is our belief *about* ourselves, while self-worth is the value we place *on* ourselves.

Self-worth and self-esteem are closely tied together and are probably the 2 most *underrated* core beliefs that we face as humans. Why underrated? Because when we master them, we become so powerful the possibilities are endless. It's when we value ourselves and know that we add value to every situation, that we have achieved a healthy balance of self-esteem and self-worth.

The unconditional love we come to this world with is evident as it sparkles in our eyes as infants. As we grow, the world is filled with nothing but wonder, until we experience something unpleasant, like being scolded for running toward the street or touching something too hot. Out of a sense of protection, our parents or guardians swat us on the behind, or tell us a firm *no*. We're too young to realize that we may get hit by a car or get burned, but nonetheless it's at that moment that we're taught that an incredible experience like running free or exploring new things is associated with pain or punishment.

Yes, there are certainly times when reprimanding young beings is necessary when trying to protect them from harm, but the scars of the adults that come to me are much deeper. It stems from the words or behavior of the people who've been entrusted to take care of them or individuals with whom they interact with in their daily lives. These people attempt to push their own fears and false beliefs on young impressionable minds. Or worse, they take advantage of their innocence, abusing them in some way, whether it be mental or physical.

Experiences shape our beliefs about ourselves. Being made to feel bad about ourselves, inadequate or not valued instills a disproportionate amount of false core beliefs about our own self-worth that we carry with us throughout our lives. It effects our self-esteem, the center of our strength.

~~~~~~~~~~~~~~~~~~~~~~~~~~~~

The people in our lives help shape our own feelings of self-worth by their actions. It's not until we stand up and value ourselves does the dynamic change. I remember the defining instance where I finally saw my value. It was at the beginning of the 1990's when I was still living and working in Washington, D.C.

I decided to surprise my mother by flying my sister, her husband and little one from Arizona to Long Island, so the whole family could be together for the holidays.

The dinner table was packed with our family and friends. After dinner, my mother made a request of my 2 sisters, their husbands and their children to all pose together, wanting to get a family photo. I sat there for a moment and tilted my head sideways. A friend sitting next to me, leaned over and whispered in my ear, "Did I just hear that right? Did your mother just exclude you from the family photo? And didn't you just pay all that money to fly your sister...." I put my hand on hers as I took a few breaths.

Then I slammed my fist on the table, the vegetables next to my place jumping out of their serving dish. "I don't believe this," I said angrily to my mother.

She turned and commented, "But you have no husband or children. I was planning of taking a picture of you separately."

There was silence in the room as I came to the realization of how my mother defined her own self-worth, through being married and having children. She had absolutely no concept of having a single daughter in her 30's with a career.

I took a couple of weeks before having one of the most significant conversations of my adult life with her. I had finally found my self-worth. I explained that if she was not going to see the value of what I have to offer and respect me, then our relationship was over. It was that conversation that would positively change our dynamic for her remaining years.

DIFFERENT WAYS OF COPING
Others Define my Self-Worth

Some people define their sense of self-worth by the values others see in them. They are concerned about what others think, continually trying to impress people by what they wear, drive, where they live or who they associate with. This behavior makes them second guess what they say and do as they doubt the actions they take to the point that it keeps them up at night.

The Grandstander

There are those who are continually grandstanding, with egos as big as houses. These people suffer from severely low self-esteem, puffing themselves up to impress others as a way to overcompensate for their own self-loathing.

The Over Achiever

The most healthy way to compensate when you have not dealt with feelings about your own strength and power are people who try hard to achieve, or overachieve in this case. I became one of these people, with the attitude of *I'll show you* striving for love and approval by pushing myself above and beyond. It had me graduate high school at 17 and achieve a 4 year undergraduate degree by 19 years old. Although the overachiever is the healthiest of this bunch, they are still searching for approval to compensate for their own doubts about their abilities.

One of my first managers, named Klaus, spotted this trait within me. He used it to his advantage to get me to work ungodly hours to achieve the unit's goals.

It was years until I finally figured out that I was looking for the approval of my own mother. Being the overachiever was like a fire that I initiated. Once lit, it could not easily be extinguished, for as soon as I would complete one monumental project, I was itching for another, always inspired to accomplish more. In hindsight, I have to thank my mother for how she raised me, since I probably would not have achieved such success so early in my career, if it were not for her.

At this point in my life, I've dealt with my self-worth issues. I no longer care what other people think of me. Some may love me, others may hate me, but it matters not. I don't measure my value by others gauge, I measure my value by my own gauge, knowing that I add value to every situation that comes along. And I don't feel the need to achieve a goal just so I can show my worth to another.

Wondering if you're there yet?

Take a moment and close your eyes and take an honest look at yourself. Gauge your response to the following 2 questions: "How do I feel about myself?" and "Do I offer value to the world?" If you start thinking that you're not good enough or have an over inflated ego, thinking that you are the best thing since white sliced bread, then you still have some work to do.

Once you have a positive self-image, believing that you're a strong loving being that adds value, it's then that all self-doubt fades into oblivion. And once you believe this about yourself, it matters little what anyone else thinks about you, making it easier to get to and maintain that ***being love*** state as you follow and act on what tickles your heart.

THE STATE OF BEING LOVE

8

NOTICE YOUR BEAUTY
AND LOVE YOURSELF

What's the first thing you say to yourself when you wake up each morning?

If the answer is not saying *I Love You* to the most important person in your life, *you*, whether an internal dialog or external exchange, then perhaps it's time to work on finding and loving that beautiful being that you are.

Are we doomed from the start?
No, but we live in a world currently full of so many negatives. Think about how much negativity that we're all exposed to daily that starts when we're children; negative patterns, speech and behavior, even if you had the best parents in the world. It's no wonder why most people don't love themselves. To reiterate, what we're exposed to during our developmental years has a profound impact on the beliefs that we carry with us throughout our lives.

The news and most television programing paint a pretty grim picture of life and the future that I call "constantly negative news" or CNN for short. It begs the question, as a society are we any less happy than before all these technological advancements?

I think the answer to that is a whopping *yes* as these continual negative depictions we experience keep us in fear. And if we're not happy, we certainly aren't going to vibrate higher and love ourselves. And if you don't love yourself right now, take a moment to ask yourself why not.

Are you worried with others will think of you?
I learned to shut off negative self-talk and beliefs and walk into that self-love by believing that it is possible to have a future where I need no one's approval except my own.

Are you lonely?
Work on cherishing those times that you *are* alone. Trust me, it's better to be content and alone than with someone and lonely. That kind of loneliness is actually worse than being by yourself. When you love who you are, then you open yourself up to interacting with people who appreciate and cherish the time they spend with you.

I decided to do this exercise and compare a time when I was living alone, though the wish to date someone was in the forefront of my thoughts, versus a time when I was dating Mr. Wrong. When I was alone, sure at times I was a little lonely, especially during the holidays, but did my best to relish this time that the Universe provided me with to work on myself. When I compare it to the few year period that I was with the wrong person, miserable, stagnant, gaining weight and not able to sleep at night as Mr. Wrong snored in bed next to me, I no longer felt sorry for myself when I had no significant other in my life. Remember that when you love yourself, you are never lonely because you are your own best friend.

Don't have a good self-image?
It does not matter if you're the tallest, the prettiest, the youngest or the most talented.

It was 2013 when I started filming the messages I had and posted them to YouTube. I had wanted to for years, but kept saying that I would do so when I was 10 pounds lighter, or had a better hair style. When I finally loved that being inside I realized that it did not matter if anyone judged my appearance because it would no longer affect me. If I had information, I was going to share it. When I first got behind the camera, I was over dramatic with my speech and hand gestures, but I knew that the information I was providing had value and that's all that mattered. At first it was a long list of videos helping people find free things to do in the spiritual Arizona town that I had made my home. As I continued to film in the places around the world that I visited, my technique got better and I no longer feared the outcome as I looked at the films for editing.

~~~~~~~~~~~~~~~~~~~~~~~

How can we get there right now?
An immediate quick fix to loving myself when I'm feeling less than stellar, is to put on some music and sing.

I remember when I was living in Washington, D.C. I did love to sing and wanted to improve my voice. Michael at work had a friend who was a singing coach and I signed up for 12 lessons. It was in that 12 week period that my heart opened and I cried, feeling for the first time in years.

It was from that point that I knew that singing was a way to open one's heart and oneself to self-love.

Sometimes the most self-healing can be obtained from singing, so never be afraid to sing when you're feeling down. It doesn't matter if you don't have a voice like a professional. You know that when you sing, the angels look down at you and smile, even if your voice sucks.

So, do it anyway. It will always put you back on track as you begin to love your true self.

~~~~~~~~~~~~~~~~~~~~~~~~

Know that you're a beautiful being, alive at this very crucial time on the planet. It's important to love the light that you are, for your illumination provides guidance to others as you move on your path.

Wake each morning with the sun, singing and in love with the most important being in your world, **YOU.**

THE STATE OF BEING LOVE

9
MAKING TOUGH DECISIONS TO MOVE FORWARD

I know that this journey we call life is filled with ups and downs. There are often times in one's life where we face crossroads and have to decide which road to travel. Which way do I turn, left or right? Or do I continue straight? These choices can fill us with indecision, fear, worry and apprehension.

Some take the road less traveled, while some follow in the footprints of others. Perhaps it's a path blazed by a relative who went to a specific school, someone you follow or a particular vocation.

In life, we're all presented with situations where we have to make decisions. And remember, even doing nothing is a decision. The choices we make will take us down one road or another as we move forward toward something. On a larger scale it happens as we decide who to marry, where to live or what career path to follow. When faced with larger decisions, some people start second guessing themselves, weighing the pros and cons. Not everyone is a maverick just jumping into the deep end of the pool. On a small scale it happens each morning as we decide what to wear or when we order our designer coffee. I've discovered that all decisions have weight, even the small ones as we move toward **being love**.

~~~~~~~~~~~~~~~~~~~~~~~~

I was at a crossroad when I was faced with a decision about where to live after the end of my marriage. I ended up moving a little over an hour away from where I had lived for several years in southern Arizona to Sedona. I was fortunate being able to work from home so I did not have to worry about switching companies. I still felt displaced, even though I had rented a beautifully furnished condominium near the base of Sedona's crimson mountains. At first I would sit there at night, lost and feeling sorry for myself. *Why didn't I fight for the house? Why did I leave all my friends?*

I had more questions than answers and perhaps left the area that had been my home since 1998 to make a fresh start. Each day I would venture out, getting the lay of the land and soaking in all that Sedona had to offer. I was looking forward to 4 seasons again, but there was this feeling of loss or more specifically being lost. It was a tough decision, but would turn out to be one of the best decisions I've ever made as I took my life in a new direction filled with joy.

DECISIONS BASED ON FEAR

When I think about making big decisions based on fear, I'm reminded of a woman named Sandra that I knew when I lived in southern Arizona. We had known each other for several years. About 2 years after we met she started dating Stefan. My partner at the time and I spent a lot of time with them. They had a very tumultuous relationship filled with continual arguing with Stefan verbally abusing her. She cried on my shoulder often and vowed to leave him. I got wind that he was going to propose and wondered how she was going to decline. When she showed up with an engagement ring on her finger, I was floored and bluntly asked her in astonishment, "You said *yes*?"

She turned to me a little embarrassed saying, "Well, I put too much time in already. I don't want to live alone and besides, I don't want to move out of his house."

I wasn't surprised that the marriage lasted less than 2 years. She walked away with what she came into the relationship with, and more verbally beaten than before she said yes. I never gave Sandra a hard time about her decision, since it is not my life, nor my path, but share this story with you to drive home the point that making decisions out of fear usually don't turn out well for anyone.

Is there anyway of deciding which road to take that may be better than the other?
When it comes to decisions, if you do so from fear based lower vibrations, you are usually setting yourself up for a large life lesson.

When you approach life from a state of **being love**, you know that you'll be guided to the best choice at that particular time. Some of my most memorable experiences and scrumptious life lessons happened when the decisions were not ones made out of fear. In the end, these decisions always end up bringing me situations more wondrous than I could have imagined.

Everyone has their own path, their own road as they proceed through life. All roads lead to the same destination. It's just that some are longer and much bumpier than others.

We've all had moments in our lives where we've looked back in hindsight and thought, *'Gee, if I hadn't made that decision, I wouldn't be where I am today.'* Yes, hindsight is 20/20, but when you take one road versus another, you never know as you're traveling, where the end result will lead you.

Each moment you can make small decisions in your day from a place of a higher vibration that lead you on the road toward ***being love***.

THE STATE OF BEING LOVE

10
CORE BELIEFS AND EMOTIONAL BLOCKS

I discussed earlier in the book that our beliefs about ourselves are solidified in our core in our early years. Identifying a core belief is like playing a mystery game as you follow clues to find Colonel Mustard in the library holding that candlestick. It's when we discover the hidden belief and bring it to our conscious mind, that we can begin to deal with it.

There's a difference between a core belief and an emotional reaction to one. Let's use the example of fear of public speaking, a fear that I needed to address as my audiences became larger. Fear of public speaking is not a core belief. It's an emotional reaction to a belief. The emotion of fear of falling on my face, people laughing at me, booing, or me losing my train of thought and the anxiety I faced with my heart pounding out of my chest and losing my voice days before I got to the podium was at times unbearable.

The core belief, however was that I believed that I wasn't good enough. That's because I didn't value myself. The belief that I was not good enough was something I added to my core beliefs during childhood.

Core beliefs like this are very common among people with low self-esteem. This same dynamic can come into play when asking for a raise from our employer, when a young man asks a girl out on a date, or the ability to speak up for what we want. We don't value ourselves and are afraid that we will experience rejection that it causes us anxiety as well as the possibility of manifesting in ourselves physically.

Be careful when identifying core beliefs, because they're often misleading. When solving a mystery we follow all the subtle clues. When we search for core beliefs we realize that they are the real reasons why we react and are triggered by people and situations. When we sift through all the emotions that present themselves when we're triggered, we peel away the layers until we find that treasure. We have to keep questioning the fear based emotions that come to the surface until we identify their root cause, the core belief. Identifying the core belief, as shown in my example of the fear of public speaking, is crucial to releasing it for good.

Negative core beliefs are created by past negative experiences and form emotional blocks that effect what we believe about ourselves.

There are plenty of experiences that people have as children that are horrific, like verbal, physical and sexual abuse, and I can relate from personal experience, but I want to preface this next story by saying that not every parent or guardian may perform horrific acts. It's *our* perception of even small events that makes us become blocked. We first have to take ownership of our perception as I provide examples of childhood trauma.

~~~~~~~~~~~~~~~~~~~~~~~~

This one in particular was when I was 3 years old, the detail of it etched in my mind so clearly. I was wearing a black jumpsuit with a silver zipper with a large ring. My grandparents were visiting our Long Island home, as they did every Sunday when I was growing up. I had to go to the bathroom and walked into the kitchen to tell my mother who was fixing the midafternoon meal, the smell of pasta and sauce filling the air.

"Wait a minute and I'll come help you," she answered.

"No, I can do it myself," I replied with determination.

I went into the bathroom, unzipped my jumpsuit and peed, pulled back up my underwear, but left my jumpsuit down. I walked back out into the living room toward the kitchen, calling to my mother. I wanted her to witness my triumph, my ability to get back into that jumpsuit on my own.

It was too late when I noticed that the front door was wide open and there stood Jeffrey, the little boy from down the street, standing there inviting me to play with him. My mother ran out of the kitchen, her face red, slammed the front door and grabbed me, scolding me as she pulled up that jumper, "I told you that you couldn't do it."

I cried and ran into my room, hardly touching my food and staying clear of my mother for a day, an eternity to a young child. I found it interesting that I was trying to gain her approval, even at that early age.

I have come the conclusion that it was that particular experience, the one that has stayed with me for these many decades that solidified that core belief within me that I was not good enough, feelings of shame and embarrassment and perhaps a couple more.

IDENTIFYING THE SOLIDIFICATION OF CORE BELIEFS
I realized that the initial situations and triggers for core beliefs are not as difficult to identify as we may think. Funny how when we get to a certain age we can't remember what we had for breakfast, but we remember a few select unpleasant experiences from early childhood in great detail, like the story I shared from when I was 3.

We all have experiences from when we are younger that if they happened to us today, we would most likely shrug or laugh them off, but to a small child, they're profound, and they shape us. I'm sure if you took a pen and paper and wrote down a sentence or two about each unpleasant experience you've had starting back to the first one you can remember, no matter how small, you would have at least 70. Although each single event may not be a deal breaker in terms of your self-worth or views of life, they build upon each other as we become the sum total of all our experiences.

~~~~~~~~~~~~~~~~~~~~~~~

I was about 4 years old when my family travelled 30 minutes to a large an indoor mall. At that time I thought the mall was its own city, everything seemed so big. I was fascinated by the small Japanese bridges stretching over ponds filled with koi.

I stood there atop one of the bridges watching the movement of the fish below me, captivated by the site for several minutes. When I finally looked up, my family was nowhere in sight.

I called out, but received no answer. It was then when I realized that I was all alone. That terrified me. My face turned white and I started to cry. I ran through the mall looking for them everywhere, but could not find them.

When I finally found them I was relieved, yet angry that they abandoned me and I was all alone.

Today if I were with family in the mall and got separated from them, I would relish the solitude and take it as a chance to explore, grab a hot caramel macchiato and perhaps indulge myself with a single piece of gourmet chocolate.

In the end I was only lost for about 20 minutes, but to a 4 year old, it was an eternity and enough of a trauma to adopt the core belief that we are alone here, separated from everyone. That core belief of being all alone in this world stayed with me until I dealt with it and released it.

~~~~~~~~~~~~~~~~~~~~~~~~~~~

When we have an experience that we find mentally painful, if we're unable to cope, we shield ourselves, by self-oppression, repression and suppression. It doesn't matter which form we use, we still cause emotional blocks.

There are several ways that people stuff their emotions, like ignoring the emotion or pretending that the event didn't happen. Some people distract themselves with obsessions with food, alcohol, prescription or illegal drugs, work, sex, gambling, exercise, the internet or television.

If this sounds familiar, know that you're not alone.

I know that emotion is just *energy in motion* and believe that there's always a physical aspect associated with emotional blocks. These suppressed feelings stay in our body; our muscles, ligaments, stomach, legs, arms, necks and head. There are a lot of theories about emotional risk factors that contribute to heart disease, one being a lack of connection and lack of intimacy with others. That doesn't surprise me as I think back to the men I have known who have had heart issues. All of them were emotionally disconnected. Trapped emotions in the long-term can cause physical illness and they remain within us until we identify and release them.

~~~~~~~~~~~~~~~~~~~~~~~~

There was a period in my life when I was in an unhappy relationship, both miserable and anxious. The doctor prescribed anti-anxiety medication which facilitated me continuing to suppress the emotions I was feeling. When my weight ballooned to over 200 pounds. I was just surviving, going through the motions, day in and day out, waiting. The more I waited, the more I weighed, as I ate to fill the numbness until my physical weight and health was effected. I knew that it was time to take action. I slowly weaned myself off the anti-anxiety pills that had kept me so emotionless. I started to feel again. Once I finally faced the emotional blocks, I started to feel better. I took steps to work on my physical weight issues. With each chunk of weight I lost, other medications I was taking were slowly eliminated from my daily regime.

~~~~~~~~~~~~~~~~~~~~~~~~

WHY WE WANT TO RELEASE BLOCKED EMOTIONS
Every unresolved emotion, self-limiting belief and
self-sabotaging act is a barricade hiding a deep
emotional pain. This pain blocks our ability to
attaining that higher vibration, that state of ***being
love***.

The clearing process begins with awareness, honesty,
and openness.

Instinctively, I knew this way back in the early 1980's
when something inspired me to write down every
unpleasant experience that I had from my youth. I
wrote volumes, journaling them into marble
notebooks, the details of these situations etched
firmly in my brain. As I did, all the feelings associated
with those emotions began to surface. I felt that hurt
and anger once again. All these little things that I had
put on that proverbial shelf was now raw, but at least
I was no longer suppressing the emotions.

There are many great tools out there that can assist us
in bringing the emotions and underlying beliefs to the
surface so we can release blockages. They all have
their merits. I found a great deal of relief from a 2
week Vipassana, but not everyone can live like a

Monk in an ashram for 2 weeks in silence meditating for over 12 hours a day. Others include Cognitive Behavioral therapy (CBT). I have become fond of the Emotional Freedom Technique (EFT)[iii] or tapping for short. It's characterized by tapping on the same meridian points derived from acupuncture, while reciting words and phrases specific to the issue to release the negative emotion causing the energy blockages that create physical ailments. When the emotion and belief are unblocked, the body's energy becomes free flowing once more.

Take the time and make your list of the small stories from your youth and find a technique that works best for you. It may just be an eye-opening experience and one that helps you release and move toward *being love*.

11

REACTION AND GROWTH

My dad was a very wise man and used to say, *let it roll, like water off a ducks butt.* For a long time I used to get angry to no end. When I would tell my dad about an unpleasant interaction with a person or a situation that I was facing or when something was eating at me, he would spout that duck saying. That just made me angrier. It took me years to discover that he was right as he tried to explain that when you're faced with challenges or someone has hurt you in some way, it's healthier not to react. He was sharing with me what he learned about life, that reacting works against our own growth.

~~~~~~~~~~~~~~~~~~~~~~~~

I remember a time when I was at a large family gathering. It was the wedding of a younger cousin and the entire family was there, celebrating their union. I was so thrilled for the bride and groom, their young faces beaming at each other, so in love. As I scanned the room, I saw my mother at a large extended table filled with about 30 of her first cousins. I went over and put my hand on her shoulder, kissing her cheek as I greeted these senior family members. My mother pressed her lips hard together as she acknowledged my presence, announcing, "You see my daughter here, she's going to be a lonely old woman."

I gulped hard and walked away, immediately moving from elation to anger to worthlessness. Tears streamed down my face. My stomach was now in knots. Questions like. *'How could she say that?'* and *'How dare you!'* and *'What did I do to deserve that?'* flooded my brain.

I allowed a modicum of cruelty, a 30 second experience to ruin my entire day. The rest of the wedding was a blur because all I could think about was that heartless statement made to everyone about me. It haunted me for years.

~~~~~~~~~~~~~~~~~~~~~~~

How we react to experiences and situations is the key to our growth as we move toward ***being love***. The key is this:

The only thing in life that we have control over is our reaction.

Seeing this in print, I hope it puts everything into perspective for you. Knowing this always gives me those extra few seconds before I make a mountain from a mole hill.

I'm not saying that I deserved the royal treatment that I received at that wedding. People come into our lives to play a role to help us move forward, testing the place where we are in our own spiritual development. When we react, we're shown the places where we still require work.

How do you react when something good happens to you?
Do you parade it around like a badge on your chest wrapped up in ego? Do you allow it to get to your head? When we react to great news in this way, then our inner growth halts.

The better reaction is to hold that joyful feeling in your heart without the *need* to share it with the world. I continually work on this since I write about my experiences, but try my best to do so from humility and a sheer wanting to help others.

How do you react when something unpleasant happens?
In the case of unpleasant situations, when we become

the victim or react in other than a **being love** state, it seems that most often the situation goes from bad to worse. When you maintain a **being love** state regardless of what you deem could be an unpleasant situation, it's then that the situation changes into something that makes the corners of your mouth curl up into a smile. And when you become aware of what can be dozens of experiences that turn from potential unpleasant situations in a single day to beautiful outcomes, then you have to wonder how you lived life being miserable for so long.

~~~~~~~~~~~~~~~~~~~~~~~~

When I was appearing in Europe, by the time I reached Poland, I was pretty much out of clean clothes. Yes, I could have used the service at the hotel, but I really just wanted to take time and perform a chore that reminded me of home, like doing my own laundry. I used Google maps to find a place close to the hotel. With a day pack full of dirty clothes, I was on my way. I arrived at the location to see that it was boarded up. I laughed to myself and thought, *"Who would have thought that Warsaw would not have laundromats everywhere like we have in the states. I guess I'm going on a grand laundry adventure instead."*

Not speaking Polish, I tried my best to ask people on the street about finding a nearby laundromat. I was directed this way, then that, each time not finding a place to wash my clothes. I had one lady send me on a 20 minute bus ride where I ended up at a dry cleaners. It was now over 3 hours since I left my hotel and when I saw the place I just laughed to myself, staying in that **being love** state. I decided that I would at least go in there and ask *them*.

I walked in and smiled as I asked if they spoke English. The woman behind the counter shook her head *no*, so I proceeded to try and communicate to her by pulling a piece of my dirty laundry out of the daypack and moving my hands back and forth as if I were hand washing it saying the word *Laundromat*. She smiled back, reached into the register under the cash bin, pulled out an address and handed it to me, saying 3 words in English, "Take Taxi there."

I thanked her and left, handing the address to the taxi driver I waved down. Within 10 minutes I finally reached my destination. I had the whole place to myself. I loaded my clothes into one of the 6 machines, then stepped out to a local farmers market across the street. I strolled around smiling, as I got a taste of the culture as well as some of the vendor's homemade creations.

After my clothes were cleaned, I loaded them into the only dryer in the place. I put in enough Euros for 30 minutes. After the buzzer rang, when I pulled them out, they were still soaking wet. At this point I just shook my head, wondering what was going on. I added more coins, looked up and thought, *"I know something amazing is going to happen, but I wish it would happen sooner rather than later."*

It was at that moment that a young woman entered the laundromat toting a large comforter. She spoke to me in Polish and when I answered her in English, she got excited and replied in the best English I'd heard since my arrival. As we chatted, she told me that she was just back home after spending 6 months in New York. She asked me what I was doing here and I shared about my upcoming appearance. We chatted for the 30 minutes that I had left on the dryer time, then she offered me a ride back to my hotel, even though it was out of her way. When we got there, she wanted to buy me a coffee and hear more about my theories. I was thrilled to spend time with her as I continued to share information, but asked her about the physical discomfort I could tell she was experiencing. She admitted that she was on her way to the dentist to treat an excruciatingly painful toothache. Working with energy and being a Reiki Master, I asked if she wanted some pain relief. With her permission, I leaned in and touched the side of her face, sharing healing energy with her for about a minute. When I was done, she cocked her head, looked at me amazingly saying, "The pain is completely gone."

I smiled replying, "I'm glad I was able to facilitate some pain relief for you, but you still need to go to the dentist." As we said our goodbyes, I knew that I was guided to share my theories about vibrating higher and help her in some small way.

What could have been a very frustrating unpleasant situation turned out to be an adventure filled with new experiences, foods and a chance to meet and help a new friend, just because of my reaction.

~~~~~~~~~~~~~~~~~~~~~~

When we think about our reaction, also think about how they may affect others. Realize that when you do not react you are not only helping yourself grow, but helping others grow by example. When you do, you are well on the road to increasing your vibration.

THE STATE OF BEING LOVE

12

FORGIVENESS

You can say that you forgive someone that hurts you, but saying it and feeling forgiveness are two very different things.

You never have to tell the person that you forgive them, because that doesn't matter. It's more important for you to feel that forgiveness within yourself. Sharing it gives it no additional weight.

I believe that we don't meet people by accident, connecting to some people for short periods to help us grow. Some of these growth spurts involve unpleasant situations. We need to forgive them for playing their part in what could be a time of our greatest transformation.

Forgiving people who have hurt you, however, does not mean that you have to continue to associate with them. A doormat you are not. If someone does not see the value of what you bring to the relationship, then darling, it is their loss.

When you can truly forgive those who have done the worst things to you, and those that have made the cruelest comments to or about you, that's when you have a good grasp on what forgiveness really is.

~~~~~~~~~~~~~~~~~~~~~~~~

I speak about *understanding compassion* in a later section of this book. It was not very long after I came to the realization that my mother's behavior was based on her core beliefs and experiences that I was able to really forgive her, and have only compassion for her. We were now living in the same state and I spent time with her, not because I felt obligated to do so, it was because I wanted to. I saw her in a different light for the first time in my life. Her frailness and fear now apparent, I was there for her in what would be the last years of her life. We talked everyday on the phone and I was able to take Friday afternoon's off so we could have a late lunch, then do something fun. When her health deteriorated, she stayed with me after minor surgeries.

When she took a turn for the worse, I spent every day at her bedside while she was in the hospital, setting up my computer and running meetings from the visitors lounge just outside her room. When they moved her to intensive care, I would sing to her even though she was in a medically induced coma, the air into her lungs from the respirator the only signs of her body's movement. I was glad that I had found forgiveness in my heart before she left this planet.

~~~~~~~~~~~~~~~~~~~~~~~~

Take a moment to forgive everyone in your life who has ever made you feel as if you're not worthy of love, filled you with disappointment or made you angry.

And don't forget to forgive the most important person in your life, yourself. For some, the hardest person to forgive is themselves, but it is crucial to moving forward, so literally, lighten up as you raise your vibration toward the state of **being love**.

THE STATE OF BEING LOVE

13

FINDING BALANCE AND CENTER

The most common way for the people I have taught over the years to find balance and center is to get into a meditative state. If you're new to meditation there are many guided meditation CDs out there. It matters not what mediation practice that you follow, as long as you get grounded, feel the connection, and bring love into your heart. This is where you'll find balance, center and peace.

MEDITATE, GROUND AND CENTER

Below are a few tips on getting to that place of peace.

Find a quiet place where you won't be distracted. Shut the blinds, light a candle and burn some incense. Remember, there's no wrong way to meditate. Whatever you experience is right.

Begin by closing your eyes. Relax and focus on your breath, feeling the air entering your nostrils, flowing into your lungs, then slowly out your nose again. Just breathe naturally, as you notice your body beginning to relax.

Slowly roll your shoulders forward and then slowly back again. Then lean your head from side to side, lowering your left ear toward your left shoulder and then your right ear toward your right shoulder.

Move your focus on the areas of your body one at a time as they begin to relax. If you get distracted, don't worry, everyone does, even the Masters. Just return your focus to your breathing, paying attention to the area from the bridge of your nose to the opening of your nostrils as you feel the air entering and exiting.

Once you feel relaxed, you'll want to ground yourself. You can do this by focusing on your First Chakra, which is located at the base of your spine. Imagine that strong roots, like those from an oak tree, are winding down from the base of your spine into the Earth. They root you to the planet and keep you grounded, helping you gain balance and center.

Now bring your attention to your Crown Chakra, located at the top of your head. Imagine that it's the most beautiful pink rose you've ever seen. With petals up, they each slowly open as you feel your crown opening, receiving loving energy from all around you.

Bring all that love into your heart and let it stay there for a few minutes, then allow it to radiate throughout your body. Once again remember that anytime you get distracted, just return your focus to your breathing, paying attention to the area from the bridge of your nose to the opening of your nostrils as you feel the air entering and exiting.

Not everyone currently meditates 20-30 minutes twice daily. Start by meditating for 5 minutes twice daily, then increasing it by a minute each day and you'll be there in no time. You just may surprise yourself as you enjoy this time and become more connected to yourself, grounded, centered and able to feel the calm. I call it being in the zone, and when I am, the entire world around me stops. My mind is not consumed by any thought. I am connected to that oneness, a peace and bliss that is indescribable.

THE STATE OF BEING LOVE

14

LIVE IN THE PRESENT

So often in our lives we have had it good, yet we can't see it because we're always looking to the future or living in the past. It's because of this that we don't see what is staring us right in the face. Everyone's life is full of pleasant and not so pleasant experiences. Both types of experiences are fleeting, impermanent.

When we live in the past we're most likely reliving an unpleasant scenario over and over in our minds, trying to alter our reaction and response. When I find myself dwelling in the past, I keep saying to myself, you can't change history so why bother dwelling on it. That usually helps me put things into perspective. The past is gone forever, so you need to let it go. If you focus on situations and find yourself getting upset or angry, then have a good cry, talk about it or write it down until you get to a place where you can put it to rest. I know when we're upset it can be difficult to easily let things go.

I've found many modalities to rid myself of that focus on the past. There are many great tools out there that can assist and they all have their merits. See the

Emotional Blocks chapter for information in techniques.

When we live in the future, we're attempting to create a scenario of what we want to happen, dangling it in front of our noses like a carrot tied to a string in front of a horse. Although it does spur us to move forward, the problem with using this technique and living in the fantasy of tomorrow, yet taking no steps to move forward toward tomorrow, then we are just distracting ourselves.

There's a healthy balance between planning toward a goal and living in a future life fantasy to the extent that it effects our ability to live now.

Yes, of course we all have unpleasant experiences, but overall most people's life could be joyful if they just took time to live in that moment and not dwell on what happened to them in the past and not look for joy in the future.

Living in the present is a delicious place to be. The present is filled with wonder and excitement of the small things we experience throughout the day. It's that gasm from that first bite into a delectable pastry, the sigh we get when we feel the sun's warmth on our skin, the smile that forms when we receive a gracious hello from a stranger or how our heart opens when we see the smile from a child. As you start living in the present, you become more grateful of those little moments that fill your day.

Another benefit of living in the present is that you're more keenly connected to what I can only describe as *information,* as you experience more synchronicity.

~~~~~~~~~~~~~~~~~~~~~~~

When I think about living in the present, I am reminded of the couple of weeks I had before appearances in Europe. I just allowed myself to let it all unfold as I stopped concentrating on where I needed to be in a few weeks. I lived each moment to the fullest. With no idea where I was going to be I found myself in Ireland, although it was never on my list. I landed in the streets of Killarney with no idea where I was going, just an idea that I was looking for a place where there was a high concentration of energy, a vortex, perhaps. Having lived in Sedona, an area filled with these energy spirals, I'm curious about vortices around the world. I stood at the corner of a small block and thought how nice it would be to find out information on an energy vortex. I closed my eyes, took a deep breath and smiled, knowing that I was fully connected in that **being love** state. I opened my eyes and looked around, guided to walk into the natural food store I saw across the street. As I walked into the establishment, I saw the cashier speaking to what seemed to be a local man.

I stood there graciously waiting for them to finish their chat. The man turned to me saying in his pleasant Irish accent, "Well now, I'll get out of your way and let you help this young lady."

He was about to exit the store and I asked him if he wouldn't mind staying for a moment, since he may have the answer to my question. Sure enough, he had the information I was seeking. He even wrote down instructions and drew me a little map before he left. The cashier commented that she was glad he just happened to stop in because she had no idea what I was asking about.

It's when we live in the present that we are open to all the possibilities, with no agenda to hold us back from experiences that further our growth.

15

CHANGE YOUR FOCUS

Sometimes you have to change your point of view in order to move toward being love.

I would be telling you a mistruth, if I did not admit that for me most times I find myself standing at the edge of a cliff looking down at the abyss and wondering, *'What the heck am I doing? How did I get here and where do I go now? Will there ever be light at the end of that tunnel?'*

I think it's those times when we are feeling so unsure and vulnerable that we are ready for our next growth spurt. I also believe that if we just take a moment to take a virtual giant step backward and see the entire situation as it has unfolded in its totality, we see it with a new and different focus; and that helps us make sense of it all.

What was so intense and less than positive, becomes an opportunity. Wow, what an interesting concept as we move forward on our journey and look to those unpleasant situations as learning experiences.

~~~~~~~~~~~~~~~~~~~~~~~~~~

I dated someone for a few months when I lived in
Sedona. He turned my world upside down and not in
a good way. At the end, I was mentally and
emotionally beaten to a pulp and probably at one of
the lowest points in my life. Even though I was away
from him, I saw no way out of the hole that I had now
dug for myself and could see absolutely no way
forward. I walked outside one evening to the
hammock on the property where I was staying and
laid there in the moonlight, crying. I had given up, but
knew that I had to find some way to shake these
feelings of despair. I threw my hands up in the air
asking to see the situation in a more positive way.

Eyes now red and swollen from the continual flow of
tears, I passed out in the moonlight one leg dangling
from the side of that hammock. As the sun started to
peek from behind the surrounding mountains, I
stirred in my resting place, feeling more alive than I
had in months. I had new enthusiasm and a drive that
I'd never felt before. I decided to have my coffee
outside and dragged my laptop along with me. I wrote
an article, then another, my hands unable to keep up
with the words that were flowing through me. I didn't
understand what was happening, but decided to keep

writing whatever was coming to me until I got tired. As I think of this time I have to say that one should be careful about what they ask for. I hardly slept for the next 8 days and at the end of that time I had the draft for my first book. Synchronicity followed with a friend handing me an editor's business card a day later.

Once I decided that it was time to change my focus from feeling sorry for myself to looking for a way forward out of the situation, something about my vibration shifted. I quickly went from being a sniffling crybaby, consumed by self-pity, back to a strong woman, a force to be reckoned with, now open to the possibilities.

When I look back on that experience, I only have forgiveness for that man who played the role of abuser in my life, at a time when I was ready for huge transformation, emerging from the chrysalis, like the butterfly, a true metamorphosis, alive in all my beauty.

~~~~~~~~~~~~~~~~~~~~~~~

Absolutely every experience is a gift that shapes us into the person that we are. I know it doesn't always feel that way when we are going through them, but when you accept that gift gladly, knowing that these experiences allow us to practice in the areas of our lives where we excel, those were we explore new frontiers or others yet where we still need to do some work to release what is keeping us from moving toward **being love,** as we accept the unique opportunity that we are provided for individual growth.

16

LIVE WITH INTEGRITY

Having worked in the corporate world and interacting with many people in spiritual modalities around the world, I've met some pretty dynamic corporate dynamos and amazing energy practitioners. I've also encountered some very successful, yet desperate people blinded by attention or money.

~~~~~~~~~~~~~~~~~~~~~~~~~

I'll never forget when I was standing in a shop in Sedona one afternoon and overheard one of the men there booking a tour over the phone for a couple to find the hidden Sacred Medicine Wheel, the Ceremonial Tepee and Mystical Labyrinth. When he quoted the price at $500 for 2 hours, I almost lost my lunch. You see, all these sacred areas are free to the public and are located behind the Walgreen's on Route 89A. It was then that I felt compelled to publish my article about how to spot a Sedona fake. I started filming all around town, posting free videos to YouTube about all the free things to do in Sedona.

I've also encountered people in the business world who will do anything for money, including lying, cheating and backstabbing.

Most people know that the knot they feel in their stomach is their wakeup call that they've steered off the path. They're doing something that's not in alignment with their true loving essence and it's that feeling that helps them realize that they need to adjust their actions. The knot signifies that they're approaching a situation from a lower fear-based emotion, perhaps greed, envy or despair.

I'm still taken aback when I encounter liars and cheaters, what some term snake oil salesmen. I guess I still have work to do when it comes to compassion for these bamboozlers, as I strive toward enlightenment.

When you live with integrity, you gain the respect and trust of others, showing them that what you have to offer adds value, enriching the lives of the people you encounter. This brings you bigger and better opportunities as more people trust you. In the long run, the rewards built on the values and actions based in integrity are greater that you can possibly imagine.

Integrity is choosing to act based on ones values rather than personal gain. It's when we strive to do our life's work in any modality and business with honesty and integrity that we're on the road to living a happy, successful existence.

From a vibrational frequency standpoint, people who live with integrity are vibrating higher as they epitomize what it means to **being love**.

The State of Being Love

17
STEPPING OUTSIDE YOUR COMFORT ZONE

Most people live within the confines of what I call a pre-determined space, with some people distracting themselves to the point that they're oblivious to anything outside that space that they've defined. *Why?* Because it's scary out there outside 2-by-2 that protective barrier that we put around us.

Some challenge themselves by trying new things. Others venture out of the country on vacation.

Going beyond that and stepping outside your comfort zone without fear is very freeing, allowing you to grow. Applauds to all of you who have taken those steps. The step itself does not have to be a giant leap, every step outside our comfort zone is a step forward. It can happen at home as we eliminate all distractions that keep us tied to that imaginary protective barrier.

When we step into unchartered territory, whether it's a journey or staying at home, not purposely distracting ourselves, but allowing the feelings to rise to the surface, that's when great transformation can occur. It allows us to stretch our wings and raise our vibratory frequency. And when we do that we take a step closer to the ***being love*** state.

I have walked with courage, reminiscing about how fearless I've been over the years on my journey and have many stories of what happens when you step beyond the 2-by-2.

~~~~~~~~~~~~~~~~~~~~~~~

One that was close to home that I recall was jumping out of a perfectly good airplane. I had been talking about doing it for years and I finally bought a tandem jump off Groupon. I'm not afraid of heights, but there was something that kept me from booking the jump until close to the expiration date of my coupon. I finally got up the courage to book it and spent time that morning meditating about the bliss I would feel as the air hit my face. I remained in that ***being love*** state.

I felt only peace and serenity from the moment I entered the skydive shop. The staff was warm, welcoming and knowledgeable. Smiles abounded from personnel and clients alike as new jumpers along with their seasoned instructors reentered the building, their experience together now complete.

The lesson was succinct for my tandem jump with my ruggedly handsome 6 foot tall seasoned Russian instructor. I was fitted with jumpsuit and harness before we went over the game plan for my experience. I listened and smiled, knowing that there was nothing to be afraid of. Any nervousness was in my own mind and I was not going to take away from my higher vibration by allowing fear to creep in.

We walked to the tarmac and my instructor turned on his wrist cam and started filming. I was very fortunate to have another instructor, a young spiritualist, his smile as wide as his heart along for the ride. He was a true reminder of my Sedona spiritual family. We three boarded the small plane and were on our way. Living in Lake Tahoe, the views are spectacular, both in winter and summer. Nothing could describe the beauty I saw as we rose about the mountaintops. I gained a view of the lake and surrounding areas in its entirety; the aqua, lapis and sapphire shades of blue of the water complimenting the harlequin green of the meadows against the dark pines.

As we neared the jump altitude, my instructor ensured that my harness was tightly secured to his as we made our way to the exit point over 12,000 feet above the land. I was excited thinking that in a few seconds I would be literally flying.

I swung my feet over the side, now part of the wind. Then it happened; I was free falling. There were no screams, just bliss and smiles. For me it was a feeling of being home, one with the Earth and sky. Words hardly describe the feeling; I was flying, weightless among the clouds, like the many dreams I had in my youth. The difference was that this was real. Free falling was almost like standing still, I hardly felt as if we were falling at all, yet I was told we were at a velocity of about 120 miles per hour. My new spiritualist friend and I joined hands on the way down, as we shared that same love of adventure.

In a few moments I felt a small jolt as the chute opened and the world slowed down to a semi-crawl. All I had to do was take it all in as my technical expert guided us to a safe landing.

I am forever grateful for this wonderful opportunity and truly blessed as I thanked the 2 incredible men whose main goal was my safety for this my first experience.

The lesson that I learned that day was to take that leap of faith, knowing that something wonderful is right in front of you waiting for you. When you step outside your comfort zone, you realize your dreams. Know that it's never too late to stretch your wings and fly!

~~~~~~~~~~~~~~~~~~~~~~~~

On the travel side, when I venture into a foreign country I only have the first few days planned and a return ticket. I stay in places that most Americans shy away from. Don't get me wrong I'm not opposed to staying at a 5 star hotel and have done so many times when I worked in the corporate world, but today I enjoy traveling more bohemian style, immersing myself in the culture. The experiences are always uplifting. Somehow they make their way into something I'm writing as well as providing the spiritual growth I continually crave.

Most people think my traveling alone, thrusting myself into a country where I don't speak the language, and allowing myself to be guided by my vibrational frequency is somewhat questionable.

I've pushed myself way outside my comfort zone many times in my life, and I can honestly say that I've been petrified more than once, at least in the beginning, but I took that first step forward because the alternative of remaining stuck in my current place was no longer appealing. It has always guided me to wondrous experiences and meeting people that I would have never met, some famous, others not, but all incredibly enlightened.

~~~~~~~~~~~~~~~~~~~~~~

I remember how terrified I was when I packed all my belongings into a storage unit, setting out for over a year on a spiritual journey to help define and solidify my theories and life's purpose. The only plan I had was for the first 2 weeks of the journey that would have me at a silent meditation retreat that was a 17 hour drive away. After that I had a couple of ideas about visiting family up north, but no real plan on where I would land. The night before leaving, I laid my head the last day in Sedona, trying to sleep. My plan was to leave at 8AM the following morning and take 2 to 3 days to travel to my planned destination. I was asleep before I knew it, but shot up in bed at 2:15 AM, wide awake. I tried to go back to sleep, yet further slumber eluded me. I shrugged my shoulders, got dressed and jumped into my car.

Now *homeless* by choice, my stomach was in a knot as I drove that first day toward Northern California. I

popped in a book on tape and just kept driving, my
hands gripping the steering wheel. I was on autopilot
and didn't realize the great time that I was making
until I reached Santa Rosa. I took a break and sat
inside a diner eating a late lunch, using their Wi-Fi to
get my bearings. I shook my head in amazement,
having sailed around San Francisco with no traffic,
and was within 90 minutes of my final destination. I
do drive faster than most people, but this on the other
hand, well, I just couldn't explain it if I tried. I decided
that it was a good idea to find accommodations for 2
nights in Calistoga, a town within 30 minutes of the
retreat. The price of all the hotels listed was
astronomical. There was no way that I was going to
pay an exorbitant price for lodging. I believed that if I
remained in that higher vibration instead of getting
upset that something would present itself. Finally I
found a listing at the right price at a resort established
at the turn of the century. It had small cottages
surrounded by over 300 acres of forestland. I wasn't
going to spring for the larger 1 bedroom cottage, but
was perfectly fine with a small room off the main
house with shared bath. It was just after dark when I
pulled up. There was a note on the door with my
name on it, a key, map of the grounds and a personal
note. I was upgraded to a cottage at no additional cost.

I was exhausted and quickly found my home for the next couple of days and grabbed my overnight bag. I was pleased as I opened the door to my accommodations to find a warm and welcoming atmosphere. A separate intimate seating area surrounded by windows in the front of the cottage housed a small stove, sink and refrigerator. To my delight was an abundance of hot water rejuvenating and healing my now sore muscles. I smiled when I saw the cherub bed skirt and enjoyed a cup of hibiscus tea sprawled on the small couch in front of the blazing fire that I created in the wood burning stove.

I woke the next morning at sunrise, renewed, yet still afraid, muttering to myself, *'What were you thinking just taking off and not having any place to come home to?'*

It was early, so I decided to quietly tour the grounds. I had no idea of the existence of this magical place before I drove down the winding road to its entrance. I walked around the immediate grounds, spying a small collection of antique farm equipment retooled as planters, and well established vines covering intimate and large group seating areas. It reminded me of the places I visited in the Catskills in my youth, with small cottages surrounding a main house. I was amazed by flowers and bushes still in bloom in late fall, their yellow and purple buds dotting areas of the property with color. This place had a spiritual twist if you looked beyond your nose at the spiritual regalia. I was provided with more than I could have imagined, a gem tucked away on 300+ acres, with its own hot spring, trails and labyrinth. I was instantly transported to a place of peace and bliss as the inspiration flowed for my writing.

When I walked up to the office I spied the following saying written in chalk on a large placard on the wall of the building:

When you walk to the edge of all the light you have and take that first step into the darkness of the unknown, you must believe that one of two things will happen. There will be something solid for you to stand upon or you will be taught to fly.
Patrick Overton

Tears welled in my eyes as I released fear based emotions that no longer served me. In that instant I knew that there was no reason to be afraid.

How was it that I just happened to be guided to this place to see that saying that would make all the difference in the world to me? I don't have the answer to that question but I was grateful that I had found a little comfort and received the confirmation that I needed to continue moving forward.

Each time I step out of my comfort zone today, I'm reminded of that saying on the wall that always motivates me to continue **being love** and moving forward.

Everyday provides us a new opportunities to move away from fear as we step out of our comfort zone toward a more enriched existence. Don't be afraid to take that first step. I'm confident you will be guided to the peace and spiritual uplift you are seeking as the Universe knows when you're ready to move forward and will provide you with guidance.

Be open to the form of the message, like my recent example, that came in a few words from a poem on the wall of a century old inn.

You just never know how that force in the Universe is going to try and get your attention and should always be open to the possibilities that lay in front of you.

18

BE LOVING WITH WORDS

Take the time to say something nice to the people you meet, thank them and say good day.

What we say has the power to make or break someone's millennium. As you move toward the **being love** state, you would never say anything that would hurt another. Actually, as you vibrate higher, you take the opportunities to help others through your words. It may be as simple as a friendly greeting to a stranger as you wait behind them at the checkout counter, or words of encouragement when you see someone struggling.

I remember a situation many years ago when my girlfriend Eileen and I ventured off into Manhattan. We were sitting in a small cafe having espresso and sharing a cannoli. I could hear an agent talking to his client, a young filmmaker, at a nearby table.

The agent was telling him that he should "throw in the towel." The agent's words were harsh and the recipient looked miserable, hunched over, his skin pale and gray, his mouth turned down and his spirit defeated. When the agent left, I excused myself, went over and whispered a few words into the filmmaker's ear. We hugged and he left the restaurant.

When I returned to my table. Eileen turned to me seeing the immediate change in this person, spouting, "Hey, that man looked like he was going to jump off the Brooklyn Bridge a few minutes ago. Now he is beaming and grinning from ear-to-ear. What did you say to him?"

"Oh, I was just sharing the love," I smiled.

"But after you spoke to him, he held his head up high, his face glowed and he was smiling wide," she replied.

I took a breath and went further, "Yes, well you would be surprised the impact you can have in someone's life in 30 seconds or less with kindness and compassion. I just reminded him of the delicious positive energy that is his true essence and not to allow someone else to convince him otherwise. It's the difference between being in a low vibration and a high vibration."

The above example rings so true. Remember, it's a poor reflection on you when your words are less than kind, so maintain your higher vibration and use your words to help and heal.

THE STATE OF BEING LOVE

19

MAKE SOMEONE'S DAY

Love shared goes a long way.

As you make your way through your day, take a moment to take a breath, slow down and notice all the people you are in contact with at work, while on the street, commuting, at the store. Take the time to help someone with their grocery bags, hold the door or let them get in front of you at the store checkout.

And go one step further and help a senior today. I have often met one of our golden year Earthy inhabitants at the market and ended up having coffee with them. You may just be the only person they visit with that month.

~~~~~~~~~~~~~~~~~~~~~~~~~

I was always the one who jumped out of bed and was dancing around, but first saw that others were different in the 1980's when I shared a house with Ellen. Perhaps back then I was vibrating the state of **being love**, at least a part of the time, but just hadn't realized it yet. She was a great roommate and a lot of

117

fun, but was struggling with depression. I'll never forget one morning when she came out of her room. I was already up for a couple of hours, appreciating the day off and greeted her smiling in a sing-song voice spouting "Good morning."

Her reply was not very nice as she snarled, "What's so good about it?"

I could have left it at that as she walked into the bathroom and slammed the door, but not this kid from Long Island, New York. I put the tea kettle on and made her a cup, light and sweet, just the way she liked it. I strolled over and knocked on the door. "What the hell do you want?" she barked.

"Please open the door," I requested. She cracked the door a little to find me holding the cup as I whispered, "I made you a cup of tea."

From that moment there was a change in her.

~~~~~~~~~~~~~~~~~~~~~~~

When I think about making someone's day I am reminded of a road trip that had me in Santa Cruz in 2013. I had a small travel notebook that was being imaged and I was waiting my turn in line by the Geek

Squad counter. The elderly man in front of me seemed distraught. His issue did not seem to be getting resolved by the clerk. It seemed that he was upset because they were loading Windows 8 and not Windows 7 onto his new machine. I tapped the man on the shoulder and offered to give him a 1-on-1 lesson right there if that would help. He smiled and we sat to the side, as I showed him how to use his new operating system. I spent a little over an hour and got big hugs from a very grateful senior. I thought it was strange that the clerk apologized to me regarding the man wasting my time, but quickly replied, "We are here to help one another. I always make it a point to make someone's day."

It's so very rare these days that we meet people who are gracious without looking for something in return. Don't forget, that we're all human and you can make someone's day by what you do. It's when you give of yourself that you transform not only yourself, but you effect the vibration of the person your helping.

THE STATE OF BEING LOVE

DO WHAT TICKLES YOUR HEART

20
DO WHAT TICKLES YOUR HEART

***Take small steps each day to do something that
provides you with joy and satisfaction***

One of the best ways to get to that **being love** state is
to do what tickles your heart. That's when you
experience fulfillment and joy that exceeds your
wildest expectations.

It starts by finding moments in your day to do
something that provides you with joy. As you find a
moment, then another, then another where you're
doing what makes you smile, then you're beginning to
vibrate higher.

You accomplish this by taking a few seconds to ask
yourself 1 question: *Is there something that I want to
do right now that will tickle my heart?*

Then do that, and take notice of the joy that you get
from it feeling grateful for that snippet of time.

A perfect example I recall one of the mornings that I
was writing this book:

- I found such joy in the 5 extra minutes I decided to stay curled up in bed, before my day got into full swing. I took time to appreciate the warmth, the feel of the covers and my foot tangled in the sheets. I smelled the fresh laundered pillowcase, allowing its fragrance to permeate my nostrils.

- I sighed as I took 10 minutes to watch the sunrise, appreciating the predawn darkness as it morphed into several colors of red and orange.

- I sat outside feeling the crispness of the early morning air, aware of the chill at the tip of my nose.

- I got excited with that first sip of that caramel macchiato as I took my time to savor the point where my lips met the cup sensing and feeling the warmth and relishing the flavor of the combination of milk, caramel and espresso in my mouth.

Keep asking yourself that 1 question all day and be aware and appreciate the feelings you have. Continue to string these moments together and pretty soon, your day is full of joyful little moments. You'll notice that when these out way all other less joy filled moments in your day is when the shift begins.

You become aware that when you start doing what tickles your heart, your routine starts to morph into more delicious events that nourish body, mind and spirit.

They lead to changes on a bigger scale, like deciding to take 20 minutes to meditate each day or perhaps taking long walks or leisurely hikes, being out in nature as you become more aware. These are great ways to connect and raise your vibration.

You do this *not* because you feel as if you have to, need to or because it's good for you. If you do then you won't enjoy the activity. You do it because you *want to* and because it provides you with fulfillment.

~~~~~~~~~~~~~~~~~~~~~~~~

I continually meet people who do things because they believe they have to, getting little or no joy from what they do. Below are a couple of examples.

There was this gentleman who took me out to lunch. During the conversation we talked about skiing. He boasted that he can get up and down the slopes 20

THE STATE OF BEING LOVE

times in an hour. At 60 years old, I was impressed, but asked him what enjoyment he gets from that. I also asked what he most appreciated about the scenery and the place where he skis.

He stared at me puzzled, stating "I push myself because it's good for me. I'm moving too fast to appreciate the scenery."

I took a deep breath as I realized that some people spend their lives moving so fast that they don't appreciate what's right in front of them.

I was speaking to another gentlemen who had his knee bound, recovering from surgery. He shared that he was a long distance runner and trains over 100 miles each weekend. I asked him what he enjoyed the most on a 100 mile weekend. He shrugged saying, "Well, I like running, but pushing myself that hard is painful, so if I have to say what I enjoy most, after the first 20 miles, it's getting the day's run over with."

I sat there thinking that he may have been missing the point, especially if he pushed himself to the point of great injury. Exercise is great for us, but doing anything to extreme is just an example of people distracting themselves for the sake of not wanting to deal with their emotions.

Little moments over times will also lead to big moments as we continue to do what tickles us. As far as big actions, I gave up a corporate position where I made a great living but lacked the enjoyment of the position. I decided that I was no longer happy and had to make a change. I'm not going to tell you that I wasn't afraid of leaving what was comfortable in search for what provided me with joy, as I took time to sum up the courage to take my life in a new more rewarding direction.

Today, I confess that I've never felt such fulfillment and joy as when I share my theories about living a joy filled life with the world.

THE STATE OF BEING LOVE

21

BEING LOVE

Your Life can easily flow and be filled with joy.
Embrace the possibilities!

Let me let you take a moment so you can let this sink in as I say it again: *Your Life can easily flow and be filled with joy.*

Out of this simple concept comes all the complexity that you want to create from it, but it's a choice and once you make that choice to bring more of that love vibration into your life, it can be that simple.

When you get to the state I call **being love** then your vibration increases and life becomes joyful. Even if you can only get there for a few minutes a day, that's a wonderful start. To get there is bigger than just a positive thought, because you have to *feel* it, so it becomes part of your core beliefs.

You've been prepared for getting to this state through the previous chapters in this book, that explain small and not so small things that are keeping you from realizing this state of joyfulness.

You also need to give yourself permission to experience the joy that has always been there, hidden from view, only because you either don't know how to get to that joy or refuse to let it in.

Most of us have been taught from a very young age about all that is not joy. We been handed a bill of goods that contradicts the very essence of who we really are, and spend most of our lives with it just out of reach, as we strive to get there by obtaining external objects or status.

Some people never move away from the illusion as they toil day in and day out reaching for the brass ring, thinking that if they can someday obtain it, the door will open and behind that door will be the joy of life they have been seeking for decades.

Discovering and revealing yourself, allowing your true self to be revealed without suffering or distraction is when you start that transformation, and begin allowing yourself to go through life in a joyful dance. You experience excitement and amazement that flows in a life that's effortless.

It's exciting as you dance around in this beautiful state of *being love* that fills your life with amazing situations and wonderful outcomes. Even when you're faced with the situations that don't seem to be going your way, if you go back to your toolset and utilize simple concepts the outcome turns from something unpleasant to something amazing.

~~~~~~~~~~~~~~~~~~~~~~~

I was coming back from several months volunteering and writing in Brazil in 2014. I had lived in modest accommodations, a couple of hours from all major conveniences. I was lucky enough to get a coach seat booked with airline miles. When I got on the plane, I proceeded to my seat with my carryon. As I got to my row I saw this man sitting in the same seat printed on my boarding pass. I of course assumed it was a mistake, because in this day of computers, it couldn't possibly have been that we both had the same assigned seat. I turned to him amicably saying, "Excuse me sir, I think you're in my seat," hoping that he understood English.

He took out his boarding pass, then shook his head no replying, "No madam, I'm in the correct seat."

We compared boarding passes and sure enough, we were both assigned the same seat. I made my way back up the aisle, waving to the first flight attendant I saw, explaining the situation and handing her my boarding pass. She motioned me to a space in the galley way. I spent a few minutes there watching other passengers getting settled as she went back to the gentlemen and investigated.

Instead of worrying about a potentially unpleasant outcome, I decided instead to focus on the juicy delicious big fat cheeseburger that I was going to have at my favorite burger joint, when I finally touched back down on US soil. It kept my thoughts light and my mouth watering. She was apologetic when she returned, asking that I follow her. She escorted me back to the front of the plane. Still with the gentlemen's and my boarding passes in her hand, she spoke with the head stewardess, who looked at them, then explained to me that there indeed was a mix-up and that this was a full flight. I was asked to deplane and wait back at the gate.

Smiling, I touched her hand as I cocked my head to one side, graciously saying. "I understand that sometimes things just happen." She handed me back my boarding pass and I walked off the plane.

As I sat in the gate area, I wondered why this was happening, but was sure that if I remained in that *being love* state, then all would turn out well. I was determined to go back to that image of the cheeseburger or better yet, the thought of soaking in a bathtub, filled with hot water, surrounded by scented candles. These thoughts put me in a meditative state as I drifted off into bliss. It was certainly better than making assumptions or becoming upset, frustrated or angry. I tried my best not to be distracted by all the other passengers that were still on line, boarding the plane.

I opened my eyes when I heard my named announced and headed for the desk. There stood the head stewardess talking with the desk attendant. She asked me for my boarding pass, which I handed over, gladly, believing that there was a spot for me. She handed me a revised one with new seat number. I walked behind her toward the plane. I didn't glance down at my new assigned seat, not caring if I was given a middle row. I was just happy to be getting on the plane.

As I entered, I looked down to find out which row I needed to find. The ticket said 1A. That's right, I was put in first class at no additional charge. And this wasn't just any first class. I was in a pod, a small room with a seat that reclines into a bed and privacy, valued at over 4000 dollars for this one way segment.

I was overwhelmed as I thanked the head stewardess and showed my gratitude and appreciation to each flight attendant that came to take my order or refill my glass. It was going to be a long flight and I took the time to share some of my experiences with them when I wasn't resting.

You would think that this experience couldn't get any better. It did. Toward the end of the flight, 2 flight attendants asked if I would come up front to the galley. I thought it was a little odd, but got up and willingly followed them. Stating that they wanted to do something for me, they asked if I would put my hands over the draining grate, then they poured left over champagne over my hands, instructing me to rub them with the sugar from the packets they handed me. Afterward, they rinsed them again with the remaining champagne. I was treated to a luxurious champagne sugar scrub with the open bottles of that $80 a bottle champagne that the crew needed to discard before we landed. My hands were smooth and it was all I could do to hold back the tears. When they were done, I hugged them both, asking, "But why me?"

"You're the most gracious and genuine passenger we've ever had. Your stories have had an effect on us.

We just wanted to share something we enjoy and do something nice for you!"

The funny thing is that I have these types of experiences all the time now, since getting to and maintaining the **being love** state.

~~~~~~~~~~~~~~~~~~~~~~~

You too can experience life as I do. Perhaps some of you have everything you want, but desire to wake each day filled with joy, looking forward to greeting the sun. I know how incredible that feels to spring out of bed and watch the sunrise over the mountains feeling grateful for my life.

- Maybe you want to stop worrying, eliminating fear, anxiety or other negative emotions from your life.

- Perhaps you want better relationships, whether it's with your significant other, family friends, or co-workers.

- Maybe you want to find more self-love and feelings of worthiness. When you're in this state, every fear-based lower vibrational frequency falls by the waist side.

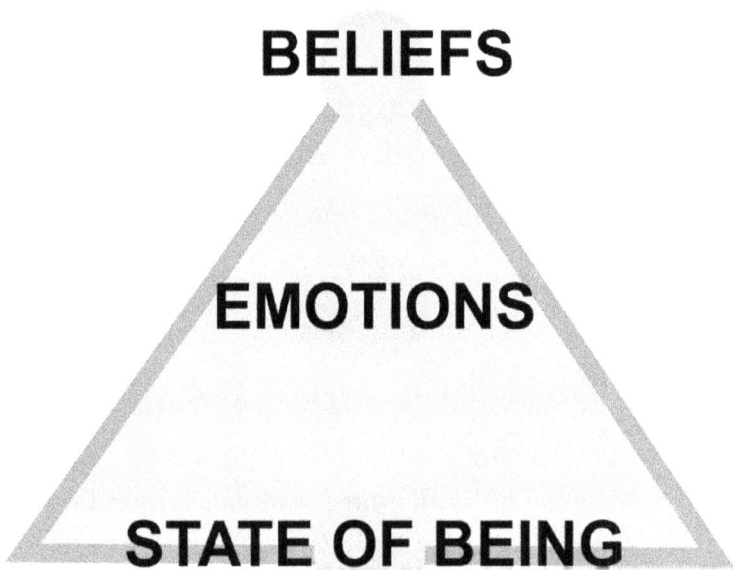

- I also mentioned that when your cells vibrate higher, it seems that your cells may rejuvenate faster. It's not only my own personal cure for wrinkles. I used to be on several mediations and today I'm on none, not even aspirin.

STATE OF BEING

BELIEFS

EMOTIONS

STATE OF BEING

©LeeZa Donatella

Your beliefs guide your perception of the world and your emotions which ultimately affects your state of being. The above triangle represents the hierarchy of how we live.

- Your beliefs effect everything in your life; your perceptions and how you interpret what you see, hear, feel and act.

- Emotions are where we hold our beliefs about everything. Emotions control the way you think, behave and act.

- Collectively they determine our state of being, what many call our vibration and frequency.

In order to get to the state of **being love**, you need to change your beliefs. Earlier chapters provide guidance on fear, invite you to move away from misery, as you work on releasing blocked emotions, eliminating guilt, as well as feelings of low self-worth and self-love. They explain ways to find center and balance, to forgive, and live in the present as you change your focus and step outside your comfort zone. Each step you take, is a step in the right direction toward **being love,** as you learn how to *not* react when others are trying to toss emotional grenades in your path. You are well on your way as you start to do what tickles your heart.

THE STATE OF BEING LOVE
The list of higher based emotions in the *being love* state includes the following

- Peace/Bliss/Joy/Happiness

- Unconditional Love

- Compassion

The goal, or for some of you the challenge, is to get through most of your day just feeling the above emotions.

And I'm going to be blunt here, and tell you that you're not going to get there if you're gossiping about another, judging anyone, yelling at the mailman or the car in front of you on your daily commute, or concentrating on who screwed you over at work yesterday. Stop being envious of what others have, get off that couch filled with despair and most importantly, keep the ego in check and stop grandstanding about the material wealth or corporate status that you've amassed.

*So how do I begin to get to this **being love** state?*

As discussed in many sections of this book it starts with the following:

- Choose to begin a joyful life, taking little steps each day to find and appreciate joyful moments throughout your day.

- Change your focus as you move away from misery and fear, and release the emotional blocks that keep you from moving forward.

- Love yourself and forgive yourself and everyone else in your life up to this point who has ever made you feel as if you're not worthy of love, filled you with disappointment, or made you angry.

- Find balance and center.

- Live in the present.

- Do not react to others, having compassion for everyone you meet, especially those who have no idea what it's like to be at this higher vibratory level.

- Practice unconditional love for every situation, even unpleasant ones, believing that something amazing will come of each experience.

UNDERSTANDING COMPASSION

I mention the 3 higher vibrational emotions that you want to maintain to get to the state of **being love**. I have provided more information about compassion and unconditional love to help you get there quicker.

It took me a long time to realize that some of the people we interact with are mere mirrors, reflecting back to us what we need to experience or practice. These people seem to be put in our path for a reason. Perhaps it's to find common connections, work together on unresolved emotional issues, or establish a new friendship. For whatever reason, most certainly it's always an opportunity to learn and grow from each other.

Knowing that we only have control over our reaction to these people's actions and no control over the outcome of the interaction, is paramount to keeping one's perspective, and staying in that higher vibration. I also know that when someone treats us in a way that's not from a ***being love*** state, then it's on them, because we're ***not*** accountable *or* responsible for the actions of others. If they're angry, frustrated, egotistical, etc., it's *their* lower vibrations of fear-based emotions that are rising to the surface.

When dealing with people who are not there yet, don't react to them, but treat them with compassion. Below is something that I think about when I'm interacting with people that are still living in lower fear-based emotions.

Imagine a 7 year old doing their math homework

I was at a friend's house watching their 7 year old while she and her husband were out to dinner. The youngster was frustrated over his math homework and was acting out. Using this scenario, let me ask you a few questions:

1. Would you react to the temper tantrum of a 7 year old you were babysitting who was frustrated over their math homework?
   Of course not.

2. Would you do their homework for them?
   No. Although you can easily complete his

homework, he would learn nothing if you did his homework for him.

3. Would you feel superior to him because you have more knowledge and experience?
   Of course not.

4. In this example you have a degree in mathematics. Would you try and explain advance math theory to a 7 year old?
   No, that would be ridiculous. He just wouldn't at this point understand.

5. So how do you help this young man with his math homework?
   Show him compassion and if you are able, provide him with some guidance that may lead him to answers.

Think of this story when dealing with the people put in your path who are still living in that misery of fear-based emotions. Do not approach them from arrogance or superiority, but with compassion as you allow them to do their homework at their own pace and skill level. And know that we all get homework in our daily life experiences. As you vibrate higher the work that comes to you will continue to challenge you to move forward.

UNDERSTANDING UNCONDITIONAL LOVE
In order to understand unconditional love I need to talk a little about both conditional and unconditional love. We learn early in our lives that love is conditional. I loved my parents when they let me stay up late, bought me that video game or took me for ice cream.

This carries over into adulthood as we love our partners if they do this or that, we love our jobs when we are rewarded with a promotion or raise, and we may even think that we'll love our bodies if we lose 10 pounds.

Love doesn't start out having conditions attached to it, since all you know is unconditional love when you exit the womb, seeing the world a new. That's what you come here with, only unconditional love. Unfortunately as we age love becomes conditional, based on our experiences.

It's when you learn how to love everything *unconditionally* once again, that you understand what true love is. It starts with loving yourself. You start to glow with a newness, just like when you were born, your eyes and skin become brighter and people comment that you even look younger. You certainly feel younger and more vibrant than you have in years.

Equally important is to love unconditionally every situation and person you encounter as you realize that each encounter and each moment has the potential to become an opportunity to let your love shine. Even circumstances that at first may not seem pleasant are turned around when you stay in that right vibrational frequency.

And it doesn't have to be some grand gesture that gets you there. I remember one time that I was at the airport during big delays. The airline staff were dealing with tons of irate passengers. I had the opportunity to share my love in the form of gourmet chocolate with some gracious airport staff one evening as I waited for my flight. They work so hard and have to deal with so many personalities that I wanted to show them my appreciation without expectation.

We're all works in progress, so don't beat yourself up for a momentary slide into a lower vibration. That's part of self-love. You have to love the person you are right now as you gain more insight and move forward. And if you want to achieve unconditional love, you first need to learn how to love yourself. When you do, then you transmute everything into love and you're no longer living in the misery of the mind, that place where all the lower vibrations dwell.

WHAT DOES THE BEING LOVE STATE FEEL LIKE

Many people ask me what does the elation that comes from attaining the *being love* state that I describe really feel like. It's a feeling of complete bliss and calm, where all is peace and love, combined with several other things, like your happy place. I know that everyone has their own happy place. Mine is a little Chihuahua that I got as a puppy named Penny. Wow, did I love that dog and when I held her my heart opened wide to the point that I could feel the love as it radiated through me. She has passed, but just the thought of her brings me to that place, because that kind of love never leaves us.

Combine that feeling with a feeling that's better than sex, more delicious than chocolate and awakens your senses to the movement of every cell in your body and you are getting close to what I feel. And the senses part, that is one of my favorite perks. Every color is more vibrant, smelling flowers or bakery items take on new layers of deliciousness, music becomes an even more heavenly experience, tastes bathe your palette with pleasure and everything you touch becomes an incredible tactile exchange.

I sometimes also get a delicious tingling wave that overtakes my body when I'm in that state, but I always feel the overwhelming feeling of peace and harmony.

HOW TO MAINTAIN THE BEING LOVE STATE

You have to know and believe that we *are* all spiritual beings having a human experience and we have the ability and deserve to have a joy filled life.

Below are tips to maintain the state of *being love*:

- The simple rule of thumb related to this state is this: When you're in that right vibration you feel warm and fuzzy inside. When you are in that *something else* state, you don't feel very good, do you?

- When in *being love*, you would never want to think, say or do anything that's not joyful, compassionate or filled with other than unconditional love. By doing so would just lower your vibration into that **something else** state.

- You love every person, animal and situation unconditionally, every single one. I've added an example in the **Understanding Compassion** section to assist anyone who's having trouble with this one.

*Why aren't we always in a state of **Being Love**?*

I won't say that a person cannot achieve a 24/7 100% connection at some point in their time here on Earth. It's certainly something worth striving for. If you can maintain this state 40% of each day, that is greater than 99.5% of the population. Imagine feeling complete bliss 40% of each day. Wow!

~~~~~~~~~~~~~~~~~~~~~~~~

When I think about moments when I needed to maintain the state of **being love**, I always love telling this story about being lost off a bus ride in Mexico. Because when I travel I make it a point to immerse myself in the culture of the places I visit and take local transit whenever possible, besides adding an extra delicious flavor to every experience, it also can have the tendency to put stress on anyone that I am traveling with, so I have been told. It was 2005 and a partner and I were spending a long weekend in Mazatlán, Mexico. He wanted to visit the marina and I insisted that we take local transport instead of a taxi. Although he was not too pleased he went along with my request. I was able to figure out which bus to take and we were on our way. Neither one of us knew more than a couple of words in Spanish, but assumed that we would see the marina as we got closer. Unfortunately, we ended up missing our stop. When the bus got to its final stop the driver basically shooed us off, leaving us in the middle of nowhere by the entrance to a beach serviced by a small bodega. There was a long tree in their courtyard that we slowly walked to. He turned to me frustrated spouting, "Now what, smarty pants?" Okay so maybe those were not his exact words, but I am toning them down for this book.

At that point I could feel his anger, but never reacted, only compassionately answering, "Well, I'm going to go into the store and get a cold drink then enjoy it under this tree. Would you like me to get you something?"

He was fit to be tied, so I allowed him to dwell in that emotion, returning a couple of minutes later with 2 cold bottles of water. I handed him a bottle, then sat down under the tree. He just sat there stewing, with me not saying a word, enjoying the refreshing cold goodness of the water as I embraced this new scenery.

After a few minutes, he lamented, "Seriously, what are we going to do now?"

Not looking his way, I simply smiled stating, "You wanted to visit the marina, right? Well in about 5 minutes someone is going to come by and take us there."

I went back to enjoying the experience knowing that the outcome would be more magical and amazing then if I had planned it.

So what happened?

In about 5 minutes a jeep pulled up. It had one of those altered rear seating areas where the benches were on the sides, instead of a single bench behind the driver's seat. A woman was in the back and they stopped in front of us. She spoke English and asked if we wanted to tour the marina. She explained that there were timeshares there and they would feed us lunch, drive us back to our hotel and give us 1000 pesos if we said yes.

My partner raised an eyebrow, hating timeshares, but I quickly corrected him, stating, "Don't worry we'll be in and out in less than an hour."

With a 5 minute ride, a free lunch and the fastest timeshare presentation in history, we received the cash and were back at our hotel.

Staying in the state of *being love* does have its advantages!

GO WITH THE FLOW

When you're in the state of *being love*, it's as if the Universe becomes your own personal concierge, making sure that you only enjoy the best experiences as you move about the world, whether it's in your own neighborhood, outside your home state or traveling internationally. Remember that your energy is part of that universal energy, so the situations and people you encounter are all like matches to your vibrational frequency, especially when you go with the flow.

It's really easy to know when you are going with the flow, because like a river as the water moves downstream, when you're in that flow, things move quickly and effortlessly.

~~~~~~~~~~~~~~~~~~~~~~~~~~

I remember when I was volunteering in a small barrio community outside San Jose Del Cabo, Mexico. I jumped in the car I rented for a couple of days to explore some of the small northern seaside towns.

I ended up at the most luxurious hotel on the small strip of beach where my travels took me, threw caution to the wind and pulled out my credit card, thinking, *'What the heck, for one evening, I would once more have a taste of the luxury afforded to me from a lucrative corporate past.'*

The room did not disappoint, with large marble tile floors and a comfortable king sized bed with six pillows and large floor to ceiling glass doors overlooking the Sea of Cortez. *'No regrets when you get that $275 dollar bill on checkout,'* I promised myself.

The restaurant view was just as spectacular and I sat down to enjoy the sunset, ordering a glass of Merlot and bowl of tortilla soup. It was then that through an interesting twist of fate, I had a chance meeting with an incredible woman. We shared stories of love and strength and the Universe worked its magic. This woman was the manager at the hotel.

She subsequently discounted my room and my meal became complimentary. Best of all I made a great new friend.

I am forever grateful for the blessings and wonderful synchronicity I continue to encounter. The only thing that could top this would be kicking back in jeans and a tee shirt sharing a beer with George Clooney at his house in Cabo or fishing with him by the arch.

I headed back toward San Jose Del Cabo a day later with a smile as I was reminded that when you go with the flow, wonderful things can happen.

GOOD OUTCOMES FROM UNPLEASANT SITUATIONS

Let's face it, we've all had unpleasant experiences in our lives or situations where we deem the outcome to be unpleasant. I think that many that go into the field of self-help do so after surmounting the obstacles of many unpleasant and harsh situations in order to help others who may be having similar life

challenges. I would be lying if I said that my entire life
has been a bowl of ripe perfectly round juicy red
cherries.

I'm not sure if life is a test of how we react to
situations to move forward, or that sometimes things
just happen. I don't believe that it matters whether or
not I ever obtain an answer to this question.

When you love every situation unconditionally and
are grateful for the interaction, that's when the true
magic happens.

A perfect example has to do with a last minute trip I
took to attend a 3 day class in Des Moines, IA. I used
one of those booking sites and landed a budget hotel
under $99 a night that also had an airport shuttle
service. My first clue that something was amiss was
when I arrived at the airport close to midnight, called
the hotel for their shuttle and was told that the
service ceased as of the prior week. My gut was
tingling when I entered the hotel lobby at 1AM to find
people at the front desk complaining that the air
conditioning in their rooms was not working. When I
finally got to *my* room and discovered that the
Internet was also not operational, I scratched my

head and shrugged my shoulders as I professed my belief about there being a pleasant outcome.

The key phrase I say to myself or out loud when I'm faced with a potentially unpleasant situation is:

> *I'm sure that there's something even more wonderful waiting for me or I'm sure that something truly amazing will come of this.*

I do this to keep my vibration in that **being love** state, not falling victim to overreacting or changing my frequency by jumping into frustration, anger or any other fear-based lower vibrational emotion like the patrons down in the lobby who were vehemently complaining to the front desk clerk when I arrived.

Because I viewed the experience as a wonderful opportunity for positive growth, I went downstairs and graciously and compassionately told the front desk clerk that I was going to seek other accommodations. He was apologetic and gave me a few suggestions as he handed me the house phone. I called over to one of the more expensive hotel that I had passed up because their rate was over $220 per night. I was upbeat as I explained my situation in the

nicest way possible and asked if they could
accommodate me.

So, what happened?

The new hotel came and got me in their shuttle as I
walked out of the current hotel free of any charges. I
was provided with an upgraded bigger more posh
room on the concierge level for $99 per night, less
than 50% of their advertised rate. The clerk went into
the back, returning with 2 chilled bottles of water,
apologizing to me for my inconvenience. To make my
stay there even more scrumptious, he waived the
Internet fees. As I plopped myself on that luxurious
bed at 2AM, I smiled, knowing how amazing things
can happen when you stay in the ***being love*** state.

Remember that you create what you vibrate and
believe. The more we stay in the ***being love*** state the
faster the resolution to potentially unpleasant
situations.

YOUR VIBRATION AFFECTS OTHERS
When I talk about how your vibration affects others, I
want you to think about a crowd of angry people and
how, like a virus, that lower vibration associated with

anger, that fear-based emotion, can quickly spread and at times even insight violence.

Or think about activists who also incite emotions that are vibrating lower than **being love** in order to get attention to their cause. Although I appreciate and support the causes, I'll never be an activist because they are not in the highest state of being.

Let's also take for a moment people who engage in firm discussions over politics. Do you see where I'm going here?

Our vibration affects others, with some like Dr. David R. Hawkins a great author who lived in Sedona, that when you vibrate love you can effectively raise the vibration of about 70,000 people.[iv] When you are not sucked into the drama of lower vibrations and remain vibrating higher, than the effect you can have on people is a positive one.

~~~~~~~~~~~~~~~~~~~~~

I was a passenger in a car as a relative was parking at a popular supermarket. As she opened her door, another car was pulling in next to her and clipped her. She became furious, got out of the car and spouted expletives toward the other driver. That immediately put the other driver on the defensive and a verbal altercation ensued, each blaming the other for the mishap. I gave them both a couple of minutes, then finally got out of the car to check out the damage as they argued a few feet away. There was no real damage here and it was time to raise the vibration of this situation for the better. After a few minutes of interjecting my **being love** state into the space, there was a huge change in the energy and emotion of both parties. All was now fine, no longer was that tension or possible threat of violence that I got wind of earlier. Everyone was satisfied and we all continued into the store.

The frequent compliment I've received over the years from people was that they loved visiting. I get so many compliments on my home. It not a grand home and I didn't have a designer. The comment I get is that my space always feels so good. Sure, it's the energy. It's like when you walk into a florist and the smell of all the beautiful flowers touches you. So does the energy when you are with someone that is vibrating higher. It just feels better.

On a grander scale, I find it fascinating watching the positive shift in the people that attend, from the beginning to the end of my lectures.

SHIFTS REALIZED WHEN YOU'RE BEING LOVE

When you're in the ***being love*** state you're vibrating so high that you're connected to something and for lack of a better term I call the energy force in the Universe.

When you are, there's the distinct possibility that you'll experience things that most of the population may consider out of the ordinary. It's an awakening from a slumber of sorts that provides you with a few more tools. The best way I can explain this is to say that there's more information and experiences in this world than most people will ever begin to realize. Over the past couple of decades I have been fortunate to experience a few.

~~~~~~~~~~~~~~~~~~~~~~

People hear me speak about the state of Goias in the center-western region of Brazil. There are incredible opportunities there for raising ones vibration.

It was in 2003 when I first traveled there for several months and was quick to realize that this was a very special place, full of energy. One town in particular was a small spiritual community in Abadiânia. I saw thousands of people from Brazil as well as other countries that had found this place, seeking different things. For many they were seeking physical healing. For me, I was seeking spiritual development and an increase in consciousness.

I was sitting in meditation with several hundred others and something was certainly happening to me as I spent more and more time in this spiritual place. As I sat there one morning, pleased with myself being able to quiet my mind to such a degree that the noise of prayers said out loud and the sounds of shuffling feet of people moved in front of me was blocked out. It was just me and my connection. About an hour into this deep connection, I was surprised by the strong scent of roses that permeated the air.

'What a delicious fragrance,' I thought, as it saturated my nostrils. *'There must be a woman passing by that's wearing a wonderful perfume.'* But the fragrance remained with me during the hours I sat there, only fading on occasion then growing more intense again. When the session ended, I saw a woman who was staying in the same lodging sitting on the next set of benches. We made our way toward the kitchen area to enjoy a bowl of soup. As we ate, we chatted about the glorious day and how nice the session was. I asked her what she thought about the wonderful rose fragrance in the room that morning.

"I didn't smell anything," she confessed. *'That's odd,'* I thought, but I let it go, assuming she must have had a cold. Everywhere I went that day that sweet rose fragrance followed me as if it were all around my head.

I walked back to my lodging, entered my room, kicked off my sandals and laid down. Within a couple of minutes once again, I smelled roses. The smell was everywhere, and so very strong that it caused me to leap from my bed and walk out into the courtyard to find the cleaning crew. I asked to smell the solution that they used to wipe down the bathroom, but it certainly did not smell like roses.

I had no idea what this was but it was starting to freak me out. It was then that I saw Ingrid, an enlightened being staying 2 doors down from me. She stood in the courtyard smiling from ear-to-ear. I walked over to her confused and she blurted out, "Smelling roses, are you sweetie?"

I was astonished and relieved that I was not going crazy, responding, "Yes I am, how did you know and why doesn't everyone else smell them?"

"That's just a Divine Fragrance and it's all around you," she said nonchalantly. I pressed her to explain.

"Roses signify unconditional love. As we become more aware and raise our vibration, our consciousness increases. Smelling a Divine Fragrance is part of aligning to higher vibrational frequencies."

At the time I didn't exactly understand the information she was trying to convey, but guessed that I was becoming more aware as my vibration increased.

"You know it was very common for the saints to smell roses," she congratulated, as she put her hand on my back.

My eyes opened wide as I spewed, "Believe me, I'm no saint, but I am very grateful to be in such a state of love." I winked and laughed, "Oh, and I appreciate being in such good *saintly* company."

It was these experiences that had me continue to search for more and more ways to discover and utilize the tools that I was being shown. I believe we all have access to these tools when we get to that **being love** state if we choose to experience them.

Even if I didn't smell roses I was certainly feeling amazing, and that would always be enough.

~~~~~~~~~~~~~~~~~~~~~~~~~~~~

Brasilia is a mecca for the spiritual traveler. I had the pleasure of visiting the Temple of Good Will (TGW), is one of those places with the largest crystal ever found suspended at the top of a pyramid type building. Underneath it is the largest spiral labyrinth I have ever seen. It is truly amazing, but the real show is the small room underneath the temple that is accessed through the first gift shop. For a couple of Reais, you can go downstairs under the temple and sit in one of the chairs and meditate. When I first visited this place at the beginning of the millennium, I looked around, saw the couple of artifacts and the large velvet upholstered lounging sofas and chairs with ottomans, and wondered what the big deal was. In later trips I would come to feel the vibration in every cell in my body as soon as I entered the room. It's an amazing place to spend a few hours in solitude soaking all that energy in.

~~~~~~~~~~~~~~~~~~~~~~~~~~~~

I don't think that this book would be complete if I didn't mention my butterfly story. I was volunteering in a spiritual town and was given permission to visit their *Sacred Waterfall* on my own. I headed down the path and entered the sacred area. As I kicked off my flip flops, I saw this very different looking butterfly perched atop the rope handrail. The texture of this insect was like one of those velvet Elvis paintings. The butterfly's body was black with one horizontal neon-orange stripe and one horizontal neon lime-green stripe painted on its back, one in each of its main body sections.

'Ah, I have an admirer', I chuckled to myself.

I was so very excited to be in this place that I began to sing a made up song of thanks. The water was frigid as I sang, smiling in my heart I splashed myself and cleansed the local crystals that I brought along with me.

As I had finished my visit, I noticed my little insect friend still sitting on the rope hand rail and smiled, including him in my song as I surveyed my surroundings one last time. I slipped my feet into my flip flops and looked up astonished to see hundreds of pairs of these butterflies now flying in a clockwise direction around the enclosed space.

They were everywhere. *'But how?'*

It took less than a couple of seconds for me to look down to slip my feet into my flip flops and back up again! I gulped in awe, now motionless. It was a miraculous moment that I still carry with me as vivid as the day it occurred. When I could finally move again, I began singing louder, in thanks, smiling as I left, hardly containing my joy, skipping all the way back up the hill. As I shared my experience with new friends I realized that it was a special gift, just for me. Over the years since this occurrence as I searched the internet, I never could find the species I saw that day in that special place.

Other Benefits
When you're in the state of *being love,* you also have profound insight, inspiration and clarity. There's also a knowing of information and any feelings of separation are left at the curb.

When I talk about insight I'm reminded of the movie *Limitless*, where someone used a drug NZT to gain total clarity. That's not necessary when you are connected and vibrating at the state of *being love*, since you can get there on your own.

The state of *being love* is like having access to universal information. It takes you to amazing places and puts you in contact with the right people at the right time.

When you are vibrating higher, you are more aware of some of the energetic subtleties that most people never experience.

~~~~~~~~~~~~~~~~~~~~~~~~

I'm continually guided to provide assistance to people in my travels. In early 2014, upon my return from 4 months in Mexico volunteering and performing research on my projects, I found myself for a day in Los Angeles.

I was dressed LA style to take time to have drinks with my friend Tone, a producer for reality TV. After our meeting I got lost on the way back to my hotel, which was over 20 miles from where we met. I never get upset when this happens, even though today I found myself driving in heavy traffic on the local Hollywood streets.

I followed my instincts and made a right at a well-known street in Beverly Hills, called Wilshire Blvd. As I drove past this incredible upscale Beverly Hills restaurant, famous for gastric infusion, something told me to turn around and go there. Having recently come from being out with my friend, I was certainly dressed well, but I was hesitant, not having a ton of cash in my pocket. I drove passed it, then was overcome by a "knowing" that I had to go there. My car practically steered itself around the block, making its way back around. As I pulled up to the valet station, I looked up and said, okay, if I am supposed to be here, my bill shouldn't be much more than $20. I laughed as I handed the valet my keys and headed into the restaurant.

I sat at one of their culinary bars where I watched the chef orchestrate tapas. I ordered a small soup and a cava (sparkling wine), trying to keep my bill to the $20 that I promised. Then something interesting happened. From the moment I walked in the door, I was treated as if I were Julia Roberts. It was the celebrity treatment all the way as I was overwhelmed by the staff's attention, including the manager.

"But, I did not order this," I shyly exclaimed, as they continually brought me delicacies from the menu. Their response always the same, "This is on us."

Funny, but as I looked around the restaurant no one else seemed to be receiving the same treatment. They brought me so much food that I couldn't eat it all. I shared a few of their delicacies with a New York businesswoman who sat beside me. It turned out to be such a great evening as I got to provide comfort to another and share a meal. I was feeling very good about this abundant experience, though still a little nervous as I got to the end of the evening, knowing that I had consumed over $200 dollars' worth of food and drink. When the bill came, it was less than $23.

It's nights like these where I am reminded that when you are in the right state of being you create a joyful life full of pleasure. This foodie sacrificed nothing as I was literally provided with life's great tastes and magically, most of them ended up to be free.

OVERCOME ROADBLOCKS TO SUCCESS

Imagine that you said that someday you're going to climb Mount Everest? And it's something that you have dreamed of doing for decades. Obtaining the goal of climbing Everest is both physically and mentally challenging and involves years of commitment. If that's your goal, what efforts have you made to accomplish it? Where are you today? Are you still on the couch dreaming, making no effort to move in that direction; no training at high altitudes, preparation and planning to accomplish this goal?

So relax, because getting to and maintaining the state of *being love* is not physically or mentally challenging. And this goal does not involve something that would have you risk life and limb to achieve.

Being love can begin today and takes the willingness to let go of all those lower vibrating fear-based emotions that are keeping you on that emotional couch, that place that still has you sitting there living in misery created solely in your mind, that illusion that life is full of suffering. You have to make an effort to get off the couch and move forward, believing in the deepest depths of your being that there's something wonderful about each moment in your day. For some of you who are reading this, it may sound like something that is unobtainable and difficult, just like climbing Everest.

Here's the big secret. It's really not.

Once you begin to acknowledge all those lower-based emotions and false negative beliefs, the healing begins, and you move forward into *being love*.

You have to want to move to a higher vibration and just like performing some physical feat, simply stating that you want to get there, but never making an attempt to actually take that first step, then another, will only have you feeling more anger, disappointment and despair.

Here's the beauty of it all; you can start right this very minute as you shed all other emotions from your life.

Living in the state of **being love** is like living each moment of each day as if you were in heaven or whatever paradise, more amazing than you can possibly imagine.

There are pieces of several movies that I liken it to. There is one where human frequencies was measured. Those people with a higher frequency were considered more aligned to the natural order of the planet. Life for them easily flowed. For example, when they walked to the train station, the train was always pulling up. They never had to look when they crossed the street because traffic seemed to continually move around them.

When you're in a state of **being love**, you live in a world shielded from a good chunk of the unpleasantness that most people face. It's as if you're living on another planet.

~~~~~~~~~~~~~~~~~~~~~~~~~~~~

I was still living in Arizona, driving on Interstate10 behind a white SUV with a ton of bumper stickers. I was running late and was in the left lane. I was close enough to read the vanity license plate that he had chosen.

When I looked in my rear view mirror, I saw the flashing lights of the police vehicle behind me. I moved over to the side of the road and got my license and registration out, trying not to get frustrated, believing that this delay was going to turn out well.

As I rolled down my window, the officer barked, "Didn't you see me?"

"No sir," I admitted.

"Do you have any idea how fast you were going?" he questioned.

"No sir," I confessed.

"Well, you were traveling more than 30 miles over the speed limit and that's a felony charge," he reprimanded.

It was at that point that I swallowed hard, but in my heart I believed that all was still going to turn out well. It was at that moment that he received a call on his hand-held radio. He confirmed, then turned to me and said, "This is your lucky day." He pointed his finger sternly at me as he handed me back my license and registration, "Now you slow down!"

I took a minute to compose myself, saying thanks to the sky, then slowly made my way back onto the highway. It was about a minute down the road that traffic came to a dead halt. I knew that this delay was not going to be a short one. I was still high on the gratitude of not getting a ticket and decided to grin as we inched forward. I said a prayer for the people who I assumed where in an accident down the road.

Then I saw it; that SUV that I was driving in front of me, in a bad accident. If that officer did not pull me over, then I would have been *in* that accident scene. Had I been protected or somehow shielded? I'm not sure how to explain it, but since it happens frequently, I no longer question it.

~~~~~~~~~~~~~~~~~~~~~

Don't let another day pass you by. Reread the sections of this book that have triggered memories of emotions that you need to release and know that you can take that first step into a more joy filled life, as you begin to awaken to the state of **being love**.

THE STATE OF BEING LOVE

[i] Hawkins, Dr David R, (2006) Transcending the Levels of Consciousness
++

[ii] My Inventions: The Autobiography of Nikola Tesla
[iii] Craig, Gary, EFT, http://www.emofree.com/
++

[iv] Hawkins, Dr David R (2006) Transcending the Levels of Consciousness